MASTERING SEO EXCELLENCE

Proven On-Page and Off-Page Strategies for Top SERP Rankings

By

ZAHEER AHMED SHAIK

B. PHARM., M. PHARM., & C.M.S.-ED

ABOUT THE AUTHOR

Zaheer Ahmed Shaik

Certified General Health & Business Consultant | SEO Expert | Entrepreneur

Zaheer Ahmed Shaik is a dynamic professional whose expertise spans multiple domains, including business consulting, search engine optimization (SEO), and health management. With years of experience helping businesses and individuals achieve sustainable growth, Zaheer has established himself as a trusted authority in the digital marketing and business consulting spheres.

A Unique Blend of Skills

Holding professional degrees in **Bachelor of Pharmacy**, **Master of Pharmacy**, and **CMS-ED (Community Medical Services and Essential Drugs)**, Zaheer's journey began in the field of healthcare. His passion for problem-solving, combined with a deep understanding of systems and strategies, led him to expand his expertise into the realms of business and digital marketing.

This unique blend of skills gives Zaheer a distinctive edge in understanding both technical and strategic aspects of business growth. He has successfully guided countless businesses through the complex maze of digital transformation, helping them optimize their online presence and achieve tangible results.

SEO Expertise and Vision

As an SEO expert, Zaheer is dedicated to empowering businesses to thrive in the competitive digital marketplace. His approach combines technical mastery with creativity and a deep focus on user intent. He has an exceptional ability to break down complex SEO concepts into actionable strategies, making them accessible for professionals at all levels.

Zaheer's profound knowledge of on-page and off-page SEO has made him a sought-after consultant for businesses seeking to enhance their visibility, improve their rankings, and connect with their target audiences.

A Passion for Education and Empowerment

Zaheer is not only a practitioner but also an educator. Through his books, consultations, and online resources, he strives to share his knowledge and insights with aspiring marketers, entrepreneurs, and business owners. His mission is to demystify SEO and equip individuals with the tools they need to succeed in a constantly evolving digital world.

Why This Book?

Mastering SEO Excellence: Proven On-Page and Off-Page Strategies for Top SERP Rankings is the culmination of Zaheer's years of hands-on experience and extensive research. This book reflects his commitment to delivering clear, actionable, and results-oriented guidance for anyone looking to master SEO.

Zaheer believes that SEO is more than a technical discipline—it's a means of empowering businesses to tell their stories, connect with their audiences, and achieve their goals. This book is his way of sharing the knowledge and strategies that have transformed the digital presence of countless clients and businesses.

CONNECT WITH AUTHOR

- **Website:** Zaheer Ahmed Shaik – https://zaheerahmedshaik.online/

- **Social Media:**

    - LinkedIn – https://www.linkedin.com/in/zaheerahmedshaik
    - Twitter – https://twitter.com/zaskdp
    - Facebook – https://facebook.com/iamzaheerahmedshaik
    - Instagram – https://instagram.com/zaheer.ahmed.shaik
    - Pinterest – https://www.pinterest.com/zaheerahmedshaikonline/
    - Tumblr – https://www.tumblr.com/zaheer-ahmed-shaik
    - Telegram – https://t.me/zaheerahmedshaik
    - YouTube – https://www.youtube.com/@ZaheerAhmedShaik-Official

- **Official E-Mail:** info@zaheerahmedshaik.online

- **Live Chat:** https://tawk.to/zas786

PREFACE

In the ever-evolving digital landscape, where competition for online visibility grows fiercer by the day, understanding and mastering the art of Search Engine Optimization (SEO) has become a vital skill for businesses, entrepreneurs, and digital marketers alike. The ability to rank higher in Search Engine Results Pages (SERPs) is no longer just a competitive advantage—it is a necessity for survival and growth in the digital world.

Mastering SEO Excellence: Proven On-Page and Off-Page Strategies for Top SERP Rankings is born from my years of experience as a business consultant and SEO expert. This book is designed to demystify the complexities of SEO and provide actionable insights to help you navigate the digital frontier with confidence and precision.

Whether you're an experienced marketer, a budding entrepreneur, or someone new to the field of SEO, this book offers something for everyone. My aim is to equip you with the tools, strategies, and mindset needed to achieve sustainable growth and online prominence.

In writing this book, I drew upon extensive research, practical case studies, and the latest developments in the SEO realm. From the foundational concepts of SEO to advanced tactics for optimizing content, building authoritative backlinks, and leveraging emerging trends like voice search and AI, each chapter has been crafted with care to ensure clarity and depth.

But more than a technical guide, this book also emphasizes the importance of authenticity, user intent, and the human side of digital marketing. Search engines are evolving to prioritize user experience and meaningful connections. As such, your efforts must align with providing real value to your audience.

Who Should Read This Book?

- **Business Owners:** Learn how to increase your brand's visibility and attract more customers through strategic SEO practices.
- **Digital Marketers:** Enhance your skill set with proven strategies and actionable insights to deliver measurable results.
- **Content Creators:** Discover how to craft content that resonates with both search engines and readers.
- **SEO Professionals:** Stay updated on the latest trends, techniques, and tools to maintain a competitive edge.

What You'll Learn

This book is structured to take you on a journey from understanding the foundational principles of SEO to implementing cutting-edge strategies. Each chapter builds upon the previous one, creating a cohesive roadmap for achieving excellence in both on-page and off-page SEO.

You'll learn:

- The art of keyword research and its pivotal role in content strategy.
- How to create high-quality, optimized content that ranks and engages.
- The importance of technical SEO in enhancing website performance and usability.
- The power of backlinks, social signals, and local SEO in building authority and relevance.
- How to adapt to algorithm updates and emerging trends to future-proof your SEO efforts.

A Personal Message from the Author

As someone deeply invested in the success of businesses and individuals, I've always believed in the transformative power of knowledge. SEO has the ability to level the playing field, allowing small businesses to compete with giants and giving everyone a chance to shine online.

This book is not just a compilation of strategies—it's a blueprint for growth, a tool for empowerment, and a step-by-step guide to navigating the complexities of the digital ecosystem.

Thank you for choosing this book as your trusted resource. I am honoured to be a part of your journey and look forward to seeing the remarkable results you achieve.

With determination and commitment, anything is possible. Let's embark on this exciting journey together.

Zaheer Ahmed Shaik
Certified General Health & Business Consultant, SEO Expert, and Author

ACKNOWLEDGEMENTS

This book is also a product of countless brainstorming sessions, workshops, and discussions with SEO professionals, business consultants, and industry peers. Their contributions and real-world insights have significantly enriched this work.

Disclaimer: All references and citations are used in alignment with ethical and professional standards. This book is intended as a guide and educational resource, leveraging publicly available information, industry expertise, and personal experience.

By consolidating knowledge from these invaluable resources, *Mastering SEO Excellence* aims to provide readers with a well-rounded, actionable, and practical understanding of SEO principles and strategies.

CONTENTS

S. NO.	TITLE	PAGE NO.'S
1.	**Introduction**	01 - 02
2.	**Introduction to SEO:** Understanding the Foundations of Search Engine Rankings	03 - 07
3.	**The Anatomy of On-Page SEO:** Essential Elements for Success	08 - 15
4.	**Keyword Research Mastery:** Finding the Right Keywords to Dominate SERPs	16 - 23
5.	**Crafting Content That Ranks:** The Power of High-Quality, Optimized Content	24 - 31
6.	**Technical SEO Demystified:** Enhancing Website Performance and Usability	32 - 39
7.	**The Role of Mobile Optimization in SEO Success**	40 - 47
8.	**Off-Page SEO Unveiled:** Building Authority Through Backlinks	48 - 56
9.	**Social Signals and SEO:** How Social Media Impacts Rankings	57 - 64
10.	**Local SEO Strategies:** Winning the Local Search Game	65 - 72
11.	**SEO Analytics:** Measuring, Monitoring, and Mastering Metrics	73 - 81

12.	**Avoiding SEO Pitfalls:** Common Mistakes and How to Prevent Them	82 - 90
13.	**Advanced Link Building Tactics for Sustainable Growth**	91 - 98
14.	**Algorithm Updates and SEO:** Adapting to Google's Changing Landscape	99 - 107
15.	**Creating an Effective SEO Strategy:** Planning for Long-Term Success	108 - 115
16.	**Future Trends in SEO:** Staying Ahead in a Competitive Digital World	116 - 123
17.	**Mastering SEO:** Final Thoughts and Expert Advice from Zaheer Ahmed Shaik	124 - 128
18.	**References**	129 - 131

INTRODUCTION

In today's hyper-connected digital age, having a strong online presence is no longer optional—it's essential. At the heart of this necessity lies the art and science of Search Engine Optimization (SEO). Whether you're an entrepreneur, a marketer, or a business owner, understanding and implementing SEO can make the difference between obscurity and visibility in the online world. With the rise of competition, mastering both **On-Page** and **Off-Page SEO** has become imperative to stand out and achieve higher rankings in Search Engine Results Pages (SERPs).

"Mastering SEO Excellence" is your comprehensive guide to navigating this ever-evolving landscape. This book is meticulously crafted to demystify the complexities of SEO and offer practical, actionable strategies that yield real results.

We begin by laying the groundwork—what SEO is, why it matters, and how it works. From there, we delve into the nitty-gritty of **On-Page SEO**, focusing on optimizing individual pages for target keywords, improving meta elements, and enhancing user experience. On-Page SEO is the foundation, but it's only half the story. That's why we dedicate substantial focus to **Off-Page SEO**, exploring how to build high-quality backlinks, leverage social signals, and enhance domain authority.

Throughout this book, we emphasize a balanced approach—combining proven strategies with innovative techniques. Our aim is to empower you with knowledge, whether you're just starting your SEO journey or looking to refine your skills.

With a dynamic blend of theory, case studies, and actionable tips, **"Mastering SEO Excellence"** equips you with the tools you need to:

- **Understand how search engines work and the factors influencing rankings.**
- **Implement effective On-Page SEO strategies to optimize your website.**
- **Leverage Off-Page SEO techniques to boost your authority and visibility.**
- **Adapt to Google's algorithm updates to maintain your competitive edge.**

SEO isn't a one-time task; it's a continuous effort. This book will not only guide you through immediate actions but also prepare you for long-term success. Whether you're an individual blogger aiming for greater reach or a large corporation seeking dominance in your industry, the insights in this book will illuminate your path.

Welcome to the world of **"Mastering SEO Excellence."** Let's embark on this journey to elevate your rankings, attract quality traffic, and achieve digital prominence.

CHAPTER 1

Introduction to SEO
Understanding the Foundations of Search Engine Rankings

In the vast digital ecosystem, where billions of web pages compete for attention, Search Engine Optimization (SEO) emerges as a crucial tool to ensure visibility, relevance, and success. But what is SEO at its core, and why does it matter so much in the modern online landscape? This chapter lays the groundwork for understanding the fundamentals of SEO and how it influences search engine rankings.

What is SEO?

At its essence, SEO is the practice of optimizing your website and its content to improve visibility in search engines like Google, Bing, and Yahoo. It involves various strategies, techniques, and practices aimed at increasing organic (non-paid) traffic to a website by ensuring it ranks higher on Search Engine Results Pages (SERPs).

When users search for a term or query, search engines aim to provide the most relevant and high-quality results. SEO ensures that your website meets the criteria these search engines use to determine ranking.

Why Does SEO Matter?

- **Traffic Generation:** Websites that appear on the first page of search results receive the majority of clicks. Without SEO, even the most well-designed site can remain invisible.
- **Cost-Effective Marketing:** Unlike paid ads, SEO focuses on driving organic traffic, making it a cost-efficient way to gain visibility.
- **Building Credibility:** High rankings signal authority and trustworthiness to users.
- **Long-Term Benefits:** Unlike paid campaigns, SEO's impact lasts longer and compounds over time with consistent effort.

How Search Engines Work

To master SEO, it's essential to understand how search engines function. They rely on three main processes:

1. **Crawling**
   Search engines deploy bots, often called "spiders" or "crawlers," to scan the internet and discover content. These bots follow links between pages, indexing content they find.

2. **Indexing**
   Once a page is crawled, it is stored in the search engine's index, a massive database containing all discovered web pages. However, not all content is

indexed—pages with poor structure, duplicate content, or technical issues may be skipped.

3. **Ranking**
   When a user enters a query, search engines analyse their index and use complex algorithms to rank the most relevant results. Rankings are influenced by various factors, such as content quality, keyword relevance, backlinks, and user experience.

The Key Pillars of SEO

SEO can be divided into three main categories, each playing a crucial role in achieving better rankings:

1. **On-Page SEO**: This involves optimizing elements directly on your website, such as:
   - **Content:** Creating high-quality, keyword-rich, and user-friendly content.
   - **Meta Tags:** Crafting effective meta titles and descriptions to attract clicks.
   - **Internal Linking:** Establishing connections between your web pages to aid navigation and distribute link equity.
   - **Site Structure:** Ensuring the website is well-organized and easy to navigate.

2. **Off-Page SEO:** This focuses on activities outside your website that influence rankings, such as:
   - **Backlinks:** Building a network of high-quality inbound links from authoritative sites.
   - **Social Media Signals:** Leveraging social platforms to drive traffic and enhance brand visibility.
   - **Brand Mentions:** Strengthening online presence through citations and reviews.

3. **Technical SEO**: This ensures your site is technically sound, focusing on aspects like:

   - **Website Speed:** Faster load times improve user experience and rankings.
   - **Mobile-Friendliness:** Optimizing for mobile devices is essential as most users browse on smartphones.
   - **XML Sitemaps and Robots.txt:** Helping crawlers understand and navigate your site.

Understanding Search Intent

A cornerstone of SEO success is understanding **search intent**—the reason behind a user's query. Search engines aim to deliver results that align with the intent, which can generally be categorized into:

- **Informational:** Users seeking knowledge (e.g., "What is SEO?").
- **Navigational:** Users looking for a specific website or page (e.g., "Google Analytics login").
- **Transactional:** Users ready to perform an action, like buying a product (e.g., "Buy wireless headphones").

By aligning your content with these intents, you increase the likelihood of meeting user needs and improving rankings.

Evolving Search Engine Algorithms

Search engines continuously refine their algorithms to improve the quality of results. Google, the dominant search engine, rolls out major updates like:

- **Panda:** Penalizes low-quality, thin content.
- **Penguin:** Targets manipulative link-building practices.
- **Hummingbird:** Focuses on understanding conversational queries.
- **Core Web Vitals:** Measures page experience factors, such as speed and interactivity.

Staying updated with these changes is crucial for maintaining and improving rankings.

The Holistic Approach to SEO

SEO isn't just about manipulating algorithms; it's about providing genuine value to users. A holistic approach integrates:

- **User Experience (UX):** Ensuring visitors find what they need quickly and easily.
- **Quality Content:** Developing engaging, original, and helpful content.
- **Ethical Practices:** Following search engine guidelines to build sustainable results.

CONCLUSION

SEO is both an art and a science. It requires creativity to craft compelling content and analytical skills to optimize performance. This chapter has laid the foundation for understanding what SEO is and why it's indispensable for achieving higher rankings in SERPs. As we progress through this book, you'll gain deeper insights into the specific strategies and techniques that can transform your website into an SEO powerhouse.

CHAPTER 2

The Anatomy of On-Page SEO
Essential Elements for Success

On-Page SEO is the backbone of search engine optimization, forming the foundation upon which successful digital visibility is built. It encompasses all the strategies you apply directly to your website to improve its performance, user experience, and relevance to search engine algorithms. In this chapter, we'll explore the critical elements of On-Page SEO, their significance, and actionable strategies to implement them effectively.

What is On-Page SEO?

On-Page SEO refers to the optimization of individual web pages to achieve higher rankings and drive targeted traffic from search engines. Unlike Off-Page SEO, which focuses on external factors, On-Page SEO is entirely within your control. It involves optimizing content, HTML elements, site structure, and user experience.

The ultimate goal is to make your website not only appealing to search engines but also valuable and engaging for users.

Key Elements of On-Page SEO

1. Title Tags

The title tag is one of the most critical On-Page SEO elements. It serves as a headline for your webpage in the SERPs and significantly impacts click-through rates (CTR).

Best Practices for Title Tags:
- Keep it concise, ideally under 60 characters.
- Include your primary keyword near the beginning.
- Make it engaging and relevant to the content.
- Avoid keyword stuffing.

Example: If your target keyword is "best vacuum cleaners," a good title might be: *"Top 10 Best Vacuum Cleaners for Every Home in 2024"*

2. Meta Descriptions

A meta description provides a summary of your webpage in the search results. While it doesn't directly impact rankings, it influences CTR by enticing users to click.

Best Practices for Meta Descriptions:
- Use actionable language and include your target keyword.
- Keep it between 150–160 characters.
- Highlight unique selling points or key information.
- Use a call-to-action (CTA) like "Learn more" or "Buy now."

3. Headings (H1, H2, H3, etc.)

Headings structure your content and make it easier to read. They help search engines understand the hierarchy of your content and its key topics.

Best Practices for Headings:
- Use only one H1 tag per page, typically for the title.
- Use H2 and H3 tags to organize subsections.
- Include keywords naturally within headings.
- Ensure your headings align with the content structure.

4. Content Optimization

Content is king in On-Page SEO. High-quality, relevant, and engaging content not only attracts readers but also earns the trust of search engines.

Best Practices for Content Optimization:
- Conduct keyword research to target the right terms.
- Use your primary keyword naturally in the first 100 words.
- Avoid thin or duplicate content; focus on original, in-depth material.
- Incorporate multimedia like images, videos, and infographics.
- Address search intent—whether informational, navigational, or transactional.

Pro Tip: Use tools like Google's **People Also Ask** section to identify related queries and incorporate them into your content.

5. URL Structure

A well-structured URL is both user-friendly and SEO-friendly.

Best Practices for URLs:
- Keep URLs short and descriptive.
- Use hyphens to separate words (avoid underscores).
- Include your primary keyword.

- Avoid using dynamic URLs with long strings of numbers or symbols.

Example: Instead of: www.example.com/index.php?=12345, Use: www.example.com/best-vacuum-cleaners-2024

6. Internal Linking

Internal links connect pages within your website, guiding users to additional relevant content and helping search engines crawl your site.

Best Practices for Internal Linking:
- Use descriptive anchor text containing keywords.
- Link to related content naturally.
- Avoid excessive linking, which can dilute link equity.

Pro Tip: Ensure that your most important pages (e.g., product pages or cornerstone content) receive the most internal links to boost their authority.

7. Image Optimization

Images enhance user engagement but can also slow down your site if not optimized correctly.

Best Practices for Image Optimization:
- Use descriptive file names (e.g., "best-vacuum-cleaner.jpg").
- Include alt text that describes the image and contains keywords.
- Compress images to reduce file size without compromising quality.

- Use responsive images to ensure they display well on all devices.

8. Mobile-Friendliness

With Google's mobile-first indexing, having a mobile-friendly website is non-negotiable.

Best Practices for Mobile Optimization:
- Use a responsive design that adapts to different screen sizes.
- Ensure buttons and links are easy to tap.
- Avoid intrusive pop-ups that disrupt user experience.
- Test your site's mobile performance using tools like Google's Mobile-Friendly Test.

9. Page Speed Optimization

Slow-loading pages frustrate users and negatively impact rankings.

Best Practices for Page Speed:
- Optimize images and use modern formats like WebP.
- Enable browser caching and use Content Delivery Networks (CDNs).
- Minimize JavaScript and CSS files.
- Use tools like Google PageSpeed Insights to identify and fix speed issues.

10. Schema Markup

Schema markup is a form of structured data that helps search engines understand your content better and display rich results.

Examples of Schema Types:
- Product Schema for e-commerce pages.
- Review Schema to display star ratings in SERPs.
- FAQ Schema to answer common questions directly in search results.

11. User Engagement Signals

Search engines monitor how users interact with your website to gauge its relevance and quality.

Key Metrics to Monitor:
- **Bounce Rate:** Minimize it by providing clear navigation and relevant content.
- **Dwell Time:** Encourage longer visits with engaging, valuable content.
- **CTR:** Optimize titles and meta descriptions to attract more clicks.

The Importance of Consistency in On-Page SEO

On-Page SEO is not a one-time task; it requires consistent updates and monitoring. Regularly review your site for outdated content, broken links, and performance issues.

CONCLUSION

On-Page SEO is the cornerstone of a successful SEO strategy. By optimizing your website's content, structure, and user experience, you create a solid foundation for search engines to rank your site favourably.

CHAPTER 3

Keyword Research Mastery
Finding the Right Keywords to Dominate SERPs

Keywords are the foundation of SEO. They serve as the bridge between user queries and the content on your website. Mastering keyword research is essential for any successful SEO strategy because it allows you to identify and target the terms that potential visitors are searching for. In this chapter, we'll delve deep into the art and science of keyword research, exploring tools, techniques, and actionable strategies to help you dominate the Search Engine Results Pages (SERPs).

The Importance of Keyword Research

Effective keyword research provides valuable insights into your audience's interests, needs, and search behaviour. Here's why it's crucial:

1. **Understanding User Intent:** Keywords reveal what users are searching for and why, helping you create content that matches their intent.
2. **Driving Targeted Traffic:** Focusing on relevant keywords ensures that your site attracts visitors who are genuinely interested in your content, products, or services.
3. **Prioritizing Content Creation:** Keyword research helps you identify gaps in your content strategy and focus on topics that offer the greatest potential.
4. **Enhancing ROI:** By targeting high-value keywords, you maximize the return on your SEO investment.

Types of Keywords

Keywords can be categorized based on their purpose, length, and intent. Understanding these types is key to selecting the right ones for your strategy.

1. Short-Tail Keywords

These are broad, one- or two-word phrases with high search volume but also high competition. Examples include:

- "Vacuum cleaners"
- "Digital marketing"

While they can drive significant traffic, they often lack specificity and are harder to rank for.

2. Long-Tail Keywords

These are longer, more specific phrases with lower search volume but higher conversion potential. Examples include:
- "Best vacuum cleaners for pet hair in 2024"
- "Affordable digital marketing courses for beginners"

Long-tail keywords are ideal for targeting niche audiences and achieving better rankings.

3. Branded Keywords

These include terms related to your brand or product names. For example:
- "Nike running shoes"
- "Apple MacBook Pro"

Branded keywords are crucial for brand recognition and loyalty.

4. Competitor Keywords

These are the keywords your competitors are ranking for. By analysing them, you can identify opportunities to compete or fill gaps in your own strategy.

5. Geo-Targeted Keywords

These are location-specific keywords, such as:
- "Best restaurants in New York"

- "SEO services in Dubai"

They're essential for local SEO and businesses with physical locations.

Steps to Conduct Keyword Research

Step 1: Brainstorm Seed Keywords

Start with broad terms related to your niche, products, or services. Think about what potential customers might type into a search engine.

Example:
For an online bookstore, seed keywords could include:

- "Books"
- "Buy books online"
- "Best novels of 2024"

Step 2: Use Keyword Research Tools

Leverage tools to expand your list and uncover valuable data, such as search volume, competition, and keyword difficulty. Popular tools include:

- **Google Keyword Planner:** Provides data directly from Google.
- **Ahrefs:** Offers detailed metrics, including keyword difficulty and SERP analysis.
- **SEMrush:** Helps you discover related keywords and track competitor performance.

- **Ubersuggest:** A user-friendly tool for finding keyword ideas.

Step 3: Analyse Search Intent

Understanding the intent behind a keyword is critical. There are three main types of search intent:

- **Informational:** Users want to learn something. Example: "How to clean a vacuum cleaner."
- **Navigational:** Users are looking for a specific website or page. Example: "Dyson official website."
- **Transactional:** Users are ready to make a purchase or take an action. Example: "Buy Dyson vacuum cleaner online."

Tailor your content to match the dominant intent for each keyword.

Step 4: Assess Keyword Metrics

When evaluating keywords, consider the following metrics:

1. **Search Volume:** Indicates how many users search for a keyword each month. Higher volumes often mean greater competition.
2. **Keyword Difficulty (KD):** Measures how hard it is to rank for a keyword. Aim for low to medium difficulty keywords, especially if your site is new.
3. **Cost Per Click (CPC):** Useful for understanding the commercial value of a keyword. High CPC keywords are often lucrative but competitive.
4. **Click-Through Rate (CTR):** Predicts how likely users are to click on a result for that keyword.

Step 5: Identify Long-Tail Opportunities

Long-tail keywords often have lower competition and higher conversion rates. Use tools like **AnswerThePublic** or the **"People Also Ask"** section in Google to discover these gems.

Example: Instead of targeting "running shoes", try "best running shoes for marathon training".

Organizing and Prioritizing Keywords

Once you've gathered a list of potential keywords, organize them into categories based on relevance and intent. For instance:

- **Informational Content:** Blog posts, guides, tutorials.
- **Transactional Content:** Product pages, landing pages.
- **Navigational Content:** About us, contact pages.

Prioritize keywords based on:
1. Relevance to your goals.
2. Feasibility of ranking based on competition.
3. Potential traffic and conversion value.

Tools and Techniques for Advanced Keyword Research

1. Competitor Analysis

Study the keywords your competitors are ranking for using tools like **Ahrefs** or **SEMrush**. Identify gaps in their strategy that you can exploit.

2. Google Search Console

Use this free tool to find keywords your site is already ranking for and optimize your content further.

3. Seasonal and Trending Keywords

Stay ahead by targeting keywords tied to specific events or trends, such as "best gifts for Christmas 2024." Tools like Google Trends can help you spot these opportunities.

4. Question-Based Keywords

Users often type questions into search engines. Incorporate these into your content to address their queries. Example: "What is the best way to clean hardwood floors?"

Common Mistakes to Avoid

1. **Ignoring Search Intent:** Misaligned content will fail to rank, no matter how optimized.
2. **Keyword Stuffing:** Overusing keywords harms readability and can result in penalties.
3. **Targeting Only High-Volume Keywords:** These are competitive and may not yield immediate results.

4. **Neglecting Updates:** Keyword popularity changes over time; revisit and update your strategy regularly.

CONCLUSION

Keyword research is not just about finding words—it's about understanding your audience and how they search for solutions. By mastering keyword research, you'll lay the foundation for an effective SEO strategy, ensuring that your content aligns with user needs and stands out in the competitive digital landscape.

CHAPTER 4

Crafting Content That Ranks

The Power of High-Quality, Optimized Content

In the world of SEO, content is king. High-quality, well-optimized content is not only essential for engaging your audience but also for satisfying search engine algorithms. Crafting content that ranks goes beyond keyword stuffing—it requires a strategic approach to deliver value, maintain readability, and align with search intent. In this chapter, we'll dive into the nuances of creating content that captivates readers and dominates SERPs.

The Role of Content in SEO

Search engines like Google aim to deliver the most relevant, useful, and authoritative content to users. Content serves as the primary vehicle for communicating with your audience and search engines alike. When done right, it achieves several goals:

1. **Increases Organic Traffic:** By ranking for targeted keywords, your content attracts a steady stream of visitors.
2. **Builds Authority:** High-quality content establishes you as a trusted expert in your niche.
3. **Drives Conversions:** Well-crafted content leads users down the sales funnel, converting them into customers.
4. **Supports Link Building:** Valuable content attracts backlinks from other websites, boosting your site's authority.

Essential Components of High-Quality Content

1. Relevance

Content should align with your audience's needs and the intent behind their search queries.

- Address specific pain points or questions.
- Ensure your content matches the type of search intent: informational, navigational, or transactional.

2. Originality

Duplicate content can harm your rankings. Create unique material that stands out.
- Conduct thorough research to provide fresh insights.
- Use your brand voice to add personality to your content.

3. Value

Always aim to educate, solve problems, or entertain your audience. Valuable content keeps users engaged and reduces bounce rates.
- Offer actionable takeaways.
- Back up claims with data, case studies, or examples.

4. Readability

Even the most informative content won't perform well if it's hard to read.
- Use simple language and avoid jargon unless necessary.
- Break up text with subheadings, bullet points, and short paragraphs.
- Incorporate visuals like images, infographics, and videos.

Steps to Crafting Optimized Content

Step 1: Understand Your Target Audience

Before writing, define your audience's demographics, preferences, and search behaviour.
- Use tools like Google Analytics to identify audience interests.
- Conduct surveys or feedback sessions to learn what they want.

Step 2: Perform Keyword Research

Leverage the insights from Chapter 3 to identify the right keywords. Focus on:
- Primary keywords for the main topic.
- Secondary keywords and LSI (Latent Semantic Indexing) terms to provide context.

Step 3: Choose the Right Format

Different types of content serve different purposes. Common formats include:
- **Blog Posts:** Ideal for answering questions or sharing insights.
- **How-To Guides:** Step-by-step tutorials for actionable solutions.
- **Listicles:** Engaging, easy-to-read lists.
- **Case Studies:** Showcase real-world examples and results.
- **Infographics:** Visual representation of data and concepts.

Step 4: Write a Captivating Headline

Your headline is the first thing users see and plays a significant role in CTR.
- Keep it under 60 characters.
- Incorporate your primary keyword.
- Make it intriguing, specific, and benefit-driven.

Example: Instead of "SEO Tips," use "10 Proven SEO Tips to Boost Your Traffic by 200%."

Step 5: Optimize for Search Engines

On-Page Optimization Checklist:
1. **Keyword Placement:** Use your primary keyword in the title, meta description, and the first 100 words.
2. **Subheadings:** Include keywords in H2s and H3s naturally.
3. **Internal and External Links:** Link to relevant internal pages and authoritative external sources.
4. **Alt Text for Images:** Describe images using keywords to improve accessibility and SEO.
5. **URL Structure:** Ensure your URL is short and includes the primary keyword.

Step 6: Focus on User Engagement

Content that keeps users on the page for longer periods sends positive signals to search engines.

- Use storytelling to connect emotionally with readers.
- Add CTAs (Calls-to-Action) to guide users to the next step.

Content-Length: Does Size Matter?

While there's no one-size-fits-all approach, longer content (1,000–2,000+ words) often performs better in SERPs. This is because:

- It covers topics more comprehensively.
- It naturally includes more LSI keywords.
- It encourages backlinks from other sites.

However, always prioritize quality over quantity. Fluff or irrelevant information can deter readers.

Visual Elements: Enhancing Engagement

Including visuals can dramatically improve content performance.

- **Images:** Break up text and illustrate key points.
- **Videos:** Engage users and boost time-on-page metrics.
- **Infographics:** Summarize complex data or processes visually.
- **Charts and Graphs:** Provide data-driven evidence.

Pro Tip: Use tools like Canva or Visme to create custom visuals that align with your brand.

Common Mistakes to Avoid

1. **Keyword Stuffing:** Overusing keywords harms readability and may result in penalties.
2. **Neglecting Mobile Users:** Ensure content is mobile-friendly.
3. **Ignoring Metadata:** Titles and meta descriptions are crucial for CTR.
4. **Skipping Proofreading:** Typos and grammatical errors undermine credibility.
5. **Overloading with Ads:** Excessive ads distract users and increase bounce rates.

Promoting Your Content

Even the best content needs promotion to gain visibility.
- Share on social media platforms.
- Send newsletters to your email list.
- Collaborate with influencers to expand reach.
- Encourage readers to share your content.

Measuring Content Performance

Track the success of your content using analytics tools. Key metrics include:
- **Organic Traffic:** Number of visitors from search engines.
- **Engagement Rate:** Time on page and bounce rate.
- **Conversions:** Leads or sales generated.
- **Backlinks:** Number and quality of links to your content.

CONCLUSION

Creating content that ranks is both an art and a science. It requires a balance of creativity, technical optimization, and audience awareness. By focusing on relevance, readability, and strategic optimization, you can craft content that not only ranks well but also provides lasting value to your audience.

CHAPTER 5

Technical SEO Demystified
Enhancing Website Performance and Usability

Technical SEO is the backbone of any successful website. While content and keywords drive relevance, technical SEO ensures that search engines can discover, crawl, and index your site effectively. It also plays a significant role in enhancing user experience, which is crucial for both rankings and conversions. This chapter demystifies technical SEO by breaking it into actionable steps and strategies to optimize your website's performance and usability.

What is Technical SEO?

Technical SEO refers to the optimization of a website's infrastructure to ensure it meets search engine requirements and delivers a seamless user experience. Key aspects include:

- Ensuring search engines can crawl and index your content.
- Improving website speed and mobile usability.
- Addressing structural issues that hinder performance.

Why Technical SEO Matters

1. **Improved Crawlability:** Search engines use bots to crawl and index content. Technical SEO ensures they can navigate your site effectively.
2. **Enhanced User Experience:** Fast-loading, mobile-friendly, and secure websites keep visitors engaged and reduce bounce rates.
3. **Higher Rankings:** A technically optimized site aligns with search engine algorithms, boosting your chances of ranking well.
4. **Future-Proofing:** Adhering to technical best practices helps your site adapt to algorithm updates and new technologies.

Core Elements of Technical SEO

1. Website Speed Optimization

Page speed is a critical ranking factor. Slow-loading websites lead to higher bounce rates and lower user satisfaction.

How to Optimize Website Speed:

- **Use a Content Delivery Network (CDN):** Distribute content across multiple servers to reduce latency.
- **Optimize Images:** Compress images without compromising quality using tools like TinyPNG or ImageOptim.
- **Enable Browser Caching:** Store static resources on users' browsers for faster load times.
- **Minify CSS, JavaScript, and HTML:** Remove unnecessary code and whitespace.
- **Choose a Fast-Hosting Provider:** Invest in reliable and high-speed hosting services.

2. Mobile-Friendliness

With mobile devices accounting for the majority of web traffic, ensuring your site is mobile-friendly is non-negotiable.

Steps to Improve Mobile Usability:

- Use responsive design to adapt to different screen sizes.
- Avoid intrusive interstitials that block content.
- Test mobile performance with Google's Mobile-Friendly Test tool.

3. Secure Sockets Layer (SSL) Certificate

HTTPS is a ranking signal and builds trust with users by encrypting data between the browser and server.

Implementing SSL:

- Purchase an SSL certificate from a reputable provider.
- Install the certificate on your hosting server.
- Redirect HTTP URLs to HTTPS using 301 redirects.

4. Crawlability and Indexability

Search engines must be able to find and index your content efficiently.

How to Ensure Crawlability:

- **Create an XML Sitemap:** List all important pages and submit it to Google Search Console.
- **Optimize Robots.txt File:** Direct bots on which pages to crawl or avoid.
- **Fix Broken Links:** Use tools like Screaming Frog to identify and fix 404 errors.
- **Avoid Duplicate Content:** Use canonical tags to indicate the preferred version of a page.

5. Structured Data Markup

Structured data helps search engines understand your content better and display rich results.

Common Schema Markup Types:

- **Articles:** For blogs and news.
- **Products:** For eCommerce sites, including pricing and availability.

- **Reviews:** To display star ratings and customer feedback.
- **Events:** To highlight event dates and locations.

Implementation Tools:
- Use Google's Structured Data Markup Helper.
- Test your markup with the Rich Results Test tool.

6. URL Optimization

Clean, descriptive URLs are better for both users and search engines.

Best Practices for URL Structure:
- Keep URLs short and meaningful.
- Include primary keywords.
- Use hyphens (-) instead of underscores (_) to separate words.
- Avoid special characters and unnecessary parameters.

Diagnosing and Fixing Common Technical SEO Issues

1. Duplicate Content

Duplicate content confuses search engines and dilutes rankings.

Solution:

- Use canonical tags to indicate the original version of a page.
- Consolidate duplicate pages with 301 redirects.

2. Broken Links

Broken links harm user experience and SEO.

Solution:

- Regularly audit your site using tools like Ahrefs or Screaming Frog.
- Replace or redirect broken links to relevant content.

3. Orphan Pages

Orphan pages are those with no internal links pointing to them, making them hard to discover.

Solution:

- Identify orphan pages using site audits.
- Link to these pages from related content or navigation menus.

4. Slow Loading Times

Slow websites frustrate users and decrease rankings.

Solution:
- Optimize server response times.
- Use lazy loading for images and videos.

Monitoring Technical SEO Performance

Use these tools to track and improve your technical SEO:
1. **Google Search Console:** Monitor crawl errors, mobile usability, and indexed pages.
2. **Google PageSpeed Insights:** Analyse and improve page speed.
3. **Screaming Frog SEO Spider:** Identify technical issues like broken links and duplicate content.
4. **GTmetrix:** Test site speed and get actionable recommendations.

Emerging Trends in Technical SEO

1. Core Web Vitals

Google's Core Web Vitals focus on user experience metrics like loading speed, interactivity, and visual stability.

Key Metrics:
- **Largest Contentful Paint (LCP):** Measures loading performance. Aim for <2.5 seconds.
- **First Input Delay (FID):** Measures interactivity. Aim for <100 ms.
- **Cumulative Layout Shift (CLS):** Measures visual stability. Aim for <0.1.

2. Voice Search Optimization

With the rise of smart devices, optimizing for voice search is essential.
- Use conversational keywords.
- Answer questions directly in your content.

3. AI and Automation

AI tools like GPT-based systems can analyse technical issues and suggest improvements quickly.

Common Technical SEO Mistakes to Avoid

1. Neglecting regular site audits.
2. Blocking important pages with robots.txt.
3. Forgetting to set up proper 301 redirects.
4. Using overly complex URL structures.

CONCLUSION

Technical SEO is a critical component of a comprehensive SEO strategy. By ensuring your site is fast, mobile-friendly, secure, and easy to navigate, you lay the foundation for success in search engine rankings and user satisfaction.

CHAPTER 6

The Role of Mobile Optimization in SEO Success

Mobile optimization is no longer optional—it's a necessity. With the majority of global web traffic originating from mobile devices, search engines like Google have adapted their algorithms to prioritize mobile-friendly websites. Mobile optimization not only impacts user experience but also directly affects your search engine rankings. In this chapter, we'll explore the importance of mobile optimization, best practices for ensuring your site is mobile-friendly, and the tools to measure and improve your mobile SEO performance.

Why Mobile Optimization Matters

1. The Mobile-First Index

Google's mobile-first indexing means the mobile version of your site is the primary basis for determining rankings. If your site isn't optimized for mobile, you risk losing visibility in search results.

2. User Behaviour

- **Increased Mobile Traffic:** Over 60% of searches are conducted on mobile devices.
- **Higher Expectations:** Mobile users demand fast-loading, easy-to-navigate sites.
- **Local Searches:** Many mobile searches are location-specific, making mobile optimization crucial for local SEO.

3. Competitive Advantage

Websites that deliver a seamless mobile experience outperform competitors in user engagement, conversions, and rankings.

Key Elements of Mobile Optimization

1. Responsive Design

Responsive web design ensures your site adapts to different screen sizes without sacrificing usability.

- Use flexible grids and layouts.
- Ensure images and media scale proportionally.
- Test your design on various devices to confirm compatibility.

2. Page Speed

Mobile users expect pages to load within 2–3 seconds. Slow load times lead to higher bounce rates and lower rankings.

How to Improve Mobile Page Speed:
- Minimize server response time.
- Enable lazy loading for images and videos.
- Optimize CSS, JavaScript, and HTML code.
- Compress files using tools like Gzip.

3. Mobile-Friendly Navigation

Navigation should be intuitive and accessible on smaller screens.
- Use clear, concise menus.
- Avoid hover-based interactions that don't work well on touchscreens.
- Include a prominent search bar for quick navigation.

4. Optimized Content for Mobile

Content should be readable and engaging on mobile devices.
- Use shorter paragraphs and larger fonts.

- Prioritize important information at the top of the page.
- Avoid pop-ups that block content and frustrate users.

5. Tap-Friendly Design

Ensure buttons, links, and other interactive elements are easy to tap without accidental clicks.

- Use a minimum button size of 48x48 pixels.
- Space elements adequately to prevent overlap.

6. Mobile-Specific Features

Leverage features unique to mobile devices to enhance user experience:

- **Click-to-Call Buttons:** Allow users to call directly from your site.
- **Location-Based Services:** Use GPS to provide local information.
- **Mobile Wallet Integration:** Simplify transactions with Apple Pay, Google Pay, etc.

Tools for Mobile Optimization

1. **Google's Mobile-Friendly Test:** Analyse your site for mobile usability and get actionable suggestions.
2. **PageSpeed Insights:** Measure page speed and identify optimization opportunities.
3. **Google Search Console:** Monitor mobile usability issues and indexing performance.
4. **BrowserStack:** Test your site on multiple devices and browsers.

The Impact of Mobile Optimization on SEO Metrics

1. Bounce Rate

Mobile optimization reduces bounce rates by ensuring users can easily navigate and interact with your site.

2. Time on Site

A mobile-friendly design encourages users to spend more time on your site, signalling quality to search engines.

3. Conversions

Streamlined mobile experiences, such as one-click purchases or simplified forms, boost conversion rates.

4. Rankings

Google prioritizes mobile-optimized sites, particularly for queries performed on mobile devices.

Common Mobile Optimization Challenges and How to Solve Them

1. Poor Loading Times

Solution: Compress media, use caching, and reduce server response time.

2. Overlapping Elements

Solution: Test your site layout on different screen sizes and adjust element spacing.

3. Content Not Readable on Mobile

Solution: Increase font sizes and adjust line spacing for better readability.

4. Non-Responsive Design

Solution: Implement responsive web design or consider a mobile-first approach.

5. Intrusive Pop-Ups

Solution: Use non-intrusive banners or time pop-ups to appear after the user has engaged with the content.

Mobile SEO for Local Businesses

Mobile optimization is especially critical for local businesses. Many mobile users perform "near me" searches with high intent to visit or purchase.

Tips for Local Mobile SEO:
- Ensure your Google Business Profile is accurate and up-to-date.
- Include location-specific keywords in your content.
- Optimize for voice search with natural language queries.
- Add click-to-call buttons for instant contact.

Voice Search and Mobile Optimization

Voice search is a growing trend in mobile usage. Optimizing for voice requires a slightly different approach:

- Focus on conversational and question-based keywords.
- Create FAQ pages to address common queries.
- Use structured data to enhance search engine understanding of your content.

Emerging Trends in Mobile Optimization

1. Progressive Web Apps (PWAs)

PWAs combine the best features of mobile apps and websites, offering faster load times and offline access.

2. Accelerated Mobile Pages (AMP)

AMP is a framework designed to create lightning-fast mobile pages. While its adoption has slowed, it can still benefit certain types of content-heavy sites.

3. AI and Personalization

AI tools enable personalized mobile experiences, such as tailored recommendations or dynamic content adjustments.

Mobile Optimization Checklist

1. Implement a responsive design.
2. Optimize images, CSS, and JavaScript for faster loading.
3. Use large, legible fonts and clear navigation.
4. Test mobile usability regularly with Google's tools.
5. Incorporate mobile-specific features like click-to-call buttons.

CONCLUSION

Mobile optimization is a cornerstone of modern SEO success. A mobile-friendly website not only improves rankings but also enhances user satisfaction and drives conversions. As mobile usage continues to grow, businesses that prioritize mobile optimization will remain competitive in the ever-evolving digital landscape.

CHAPTER 7

Off-Page SEO Unveiled

Building Authority Through Backlinks

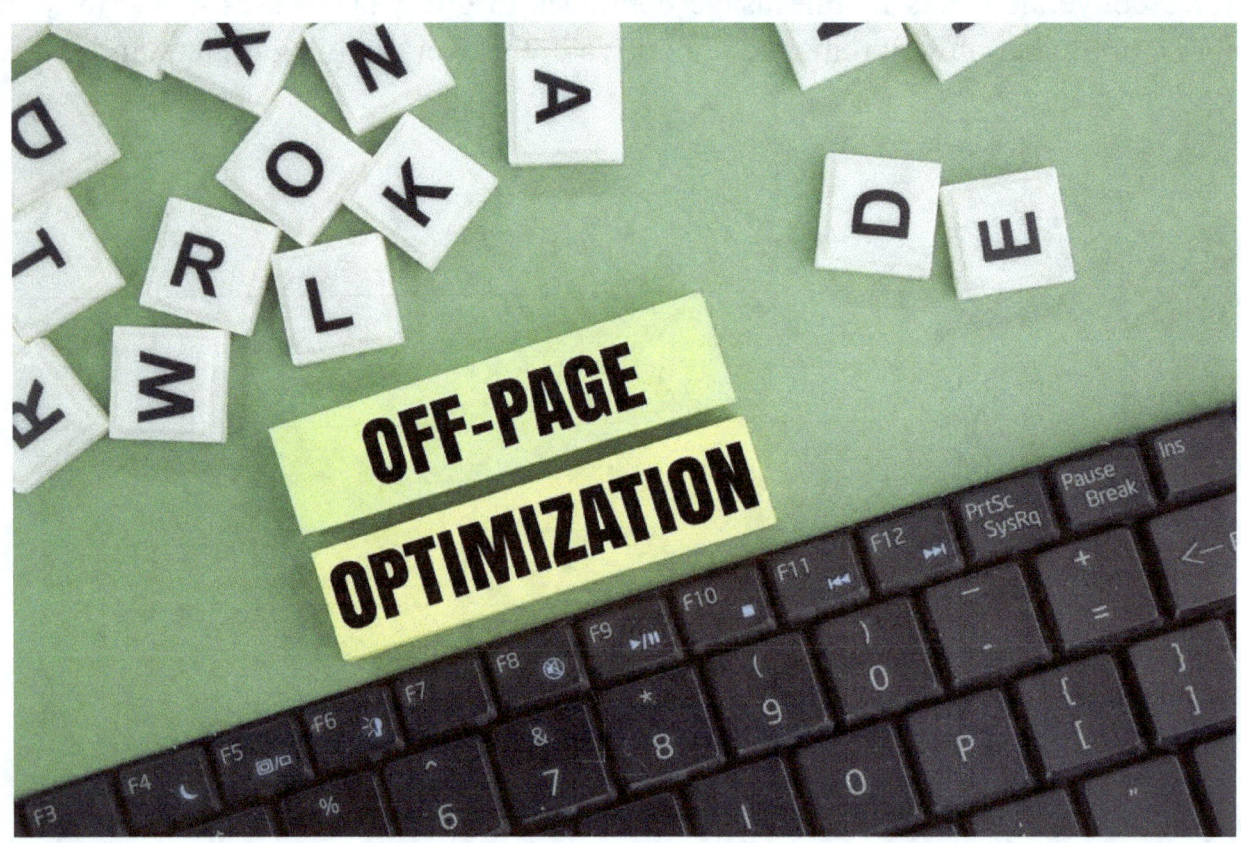

Off-page SEO is the secret sauce behind a website's authority, trustworthiness, and relevance in the vast digital ecosystem. While on-page SEO focuses on optimizing elements within your website, off-page SEO revolves around activities performed outside of your site to enhance its visibility, credibility, and domain authority. Central to this strategy are backlinks—hyperlinks from external websites that point to your pages. In this chapter, we will uncover the intricacies of off-page SEO and provide actionable strategies to build high-quality backlinks that boost your site's rankings and overall presence.

What is Off-Page SEO?

Off-page SEO encompasses all efforts outside your website aimed at improving its search engine ranking and authority. It includes:

- **Backlink Building:** Acquiring links from other sites to enhance your site's credibility.
- **Brand Mentions:** Earning unlinked mentions across the web.
- **Social Media Engagement:** Using social platforms to increase awareness and drive traffic.
- **Local SEO Practices:** Optimizing your online presence for local searches, including Google Business Profile optimization.

These strategies collectively signal to search engines that your website is valuable, trustworthy, and relevant to users.

Why Are Backlinks So Important?

Backlinks are considered the backbone of off-page SEO for several reasons:

1. Authority and Trust

Backlinks from reputable websites act as endorsements, indicating that your site provides valuable content.

2. Referral Traffic

Quality backlinks from high-traffic sites can drive significant visitors to your website.

3. Enhanced Search Rankings

Google's algorithm considers backlinks a crucial ranking factor. Sites with high-quality backlinks often rank higher.

4. Networking Opportunities

Collaborating with authoritative sites opens doors to partnerships, guest posts, and shared audiences.

Types of Backlinks

Not all backlinks are created equal. Understanding their types helps you prioritize quality over quantity.

1. Do-Follow Backlinks

These links pass link equity (or "link juice") to your site, improving its authority and rankings.

2. No-Follow Backlinks

No-follow links don't pass link equity but can still drive traffic and brand exposure.

3. Editorial Backlinks

These are earned naturally when other sites link to your high-quality content as a reference.

4. Guest Post Backlinks

Backlinks you include within articles written for other websites.

5. Directory Links

Links obtained by listing your site in reputable directories, particularly for local businesses.

6. Contextual Backlinks

Links placed within relevant content, offering the highest value for SEO.

Strategies for Building High-Quality Backlinks

1. Create Exceptional Content

Content that is informative, unique, and engaging naturally attracts backlinks. Consider creating:

- Comprehensive guides.
- Original research and case studies.
- Infographics and visual content.
- Videos and webinars.

2. Leverage Guest Posting

Writing for reputable websites in your niche helps you earn contextual backlinks and reach new audiences.

Steps to Execute a Guest Post Strategy:
- Identify authoritative blogs in your niche.
- Pitch a unique and valuable topic idea.
- Write high-quality, non-promotional content.
- Include a backlink to a relevant page on your site.

3. Build Relationships

Networking within your industry fosters collaborations and backlink opportunities.
- Engage with influencers and thought leaders.
- Participate in online forums and communities.
- Partner with complementary businesses for cross-promotion.

4. Broken Link Building

This strategy involves identifying broken links on other websites and offering your content as a replacement.

How to Implement Broken Link Building:
1. Use tools like Ahrefs or SEMrush to find broken links on relevant websites.
2. Create or repurpose content to match the broken link's topic.
3. Reach out to the site owner with a polite request to replace the link.

5. Skyscraper Technique

This involves creating superior content compared to existing high-ranking pages and promoting it to earn backlinks.

Steps for the Skyscraper Technique:
1. Identify popular content in your niche using tools like BuzzSumo.
2. Create a more detailed, updated, or visually appealing version.
3. Reach out to sites linking to the original content and pitch your piece as a better alternative.

6. Utilize Social Media

While social media links are typically no-follow, they amplify your content's reach, increasing its chances of earning backlinks.

- Share your content on platforms where your audience is active.
- Engage with followers to foster a community.
- Collaborate with influencers for increased visibility.

7. Local SEO Directories

Register your business on platforms like Google Business Profile, Yelp, and industry-specific directories to gain valuable backlinks.

Tools to Enhance Your Backlink Strategy

1. Ahrefs

Monitor your backlink profile, identify opportunities, and analyse competitors' link-building strategies.

2. SEMrush

Track your site's authority score, check for toxic backlinks, and uncover outreach opportunities.

3. Moz Link Explorer

Measure link metrics, including domain authority (DA) and page authority (PA).

4. BuzzSumo

Discover content ideas and influencers in your niche.

5. Google Search Console

Identify backlinks pointing to your site and monitor their performance.

Avoiding Toxic Backlinks

Not all backlinks are beneficial. Low-quality or "toxic" backlinks can harm your SEO.

How to Spot Toxic Backlinks:

- Links from spammy, irrelevant, or penalized sites.
- Links created through black-hat SEO techniques.
- Excessive backlinks with over-optimized anchor text.

How to Disavow Toxic Backlinks:

- Use Google Search Console to download your backlink profile.
- Identify harmful links.
- Create a disavow file and upload it to Google to exclude those links from affecting your rankings.

Measuring Backlink Performance

To ensure your link-building efforts yield results, track these metrics:

- **Domain Authority (DA):** The overall authority of linking domains.
- **Referral Traffic:** Visitors arriving via backlinks.
- **Anchor Text Distribution:** Ensure diversity in anchor text to avoid penalties.
- **Number of Linking Domains:** More referring domains signal credibility.

The Future of Off-Page SEO

1. Evolving Link Valuation

Search engines are becoming better at identifying natural, high-quality links.

2. Brand Mentions as a Ranking Signal

Unlinked brand mentions may become a more significant ranking factor.

3. AI and Predictive Analytics

AI tools will enable more precise targeting of link-building opportunities.

CONCLUSION

Off-page SEO, particularly backlink building, is vital for establishing your website's authority and achieving higher rankings. By focusing on quality over quantity, leveraging diverse strategies, and staying updated on best practices, you can develop a robust off-page SEO strategy that withstands algorithm updates and enhances your digital presence.

CHAPTER 8

Social Signals and SEO
How Social Media Impacts Rankings

In the world of digital marketing, social media is a force to be reckoned with. It serves as a powerful tool for branding, engagement, and traffic generation. But how does social media impact search engine rankings? The concept of "social signals" refers to the engagement metrics—likes, shares, comments, and overall activity—generated by social media content. While search engines like Google do not directly consider these signals in their algorithms, social media has an indirect yet substantial influence on your SEO performance.

This chapter explores the relationship between social media and SEO, providing actionable strategies to use social platforms to enhance your rankings and overall online presence.

Understanding Social Signals in SEO

Social signals are activities and engagements on your social media posts, such as:

- **Likes and Reactions**
- **Shares and Retweets**
- **Comments and Replies**
- **Mentions and Hashtags**

These signals do not directly improve rankings but act as a catalyst by increasing content visibility, driving traffic, and fostering backlinks.

The Indirect Impact of Social Signals on SEO

1. Increased Content Visibility

When your content is widely shared on social media, it reaches a broader audience, increasing the chances of it being linked by other websites.

2. Enhanced Brand Awareness

A strong social media presence builds brand recognition and trust, which can indirectly lead to higher click-through rates (CTR) in search engine results.

3. Boosted Referral Traffic

Social media platforms drive significant referral traffic to your site, signalling to search engines that your content is valuable and relevant.

4. Encouragement of Backlinks

Popular social media content often attracts backlinks from blogs, news outlets, and industry influencers.

5. Influence on Personalized Search Results

Search engines like Google consider user behaviour, including social activity, to personalize search results.

Social Media Platforms That Impact SEO the Most

1. Facebook

With billions of active users, Facebook is a prime platform for sharing content and engaging audiences.

SEO Tips for Facebook:
- Post high-quality, engaging content consistently.
- Use visuals like infographics, images, and videos to boost shares.
- Encourage comments and discussions to increase post visibility.

2. Twitter

Twitter is ideal for real-time engagement and sharing concise, impactful content.

SEO Tips for Twitter:
- Use relevant hashtags to increase discoverability.
- Engage with industry influencers to amplify your content.

- Share links to your website with compelling captions.

3. LinkedIn

LinkedIn is a professional network that excels in B2B marketing and thought leadership.

SEO Tips for LinkedIn:
- Publish in-depth articles and updates to establish authority.
- Share industry news and insights to foster engagement.
- Optimize your company page with relevant keywords.

4. Instagram

Although less link-focused, Instagram enhances brand visibility through visuals and storytelling.

SEO Tips for Instagram:
- Use stories, reels, and posts to showcase your brand's personality.
- Include links in your bio and stories to drive traffic.
- Leverage hashtags to reach a broader audience.

5. Pinterest

A visual discovery platform, Pinterest is excellent for driving referral traffic.

SEO Tips for Pinterest:
- Create keyword-optimized pins with visually appealing images.
- Link your pins to relevant pages on your website.
- Use rich pins to provide more context to your content.

How to Optimize Social Media for SEO

1. Share High-Quality Content

Your social media content should be informative, engaging, and shareable.
- Focus on solving problems or answering questions.
- Include compelling visuals and attention-grabbing headlines.

2. Build a Consistent Posting Schedule

Regular activity keeps your audience engaged and increases your reach. Use tools like Buffer or Hootsuite to schedule posts.

3. Optimize Social Media Profiles

Ensure your profiles reflect your brand identity and contain relevant keywords.
- Use a clear and professional profile picture or logo.
- Write a concise, keyword-rich bio.
- Include a link to your website.

4. Encourage Engagement

Prompt your audience to like, comment, and share your posts. Engagement increases visibility in social media algorithms.

- Ask questions or create polls.
- Respond to comments promptly to build a sense of community.

5. Use Social Media Ads

Promoted posts or ads help you reach a targeted audience, driving more traffic to your content.

Measuring Social Signals and Their SEO Impact

1. Key Metrics to Track:
- Number of shares, likes, and comments.
- Referral traffic from social media.
- Social engagement rate (total engagement divided by reach).
- Growth in backlinks originating from shared content.

2. Tools to Monitor Performance:
- **Google Analytics:** Track referral traffic and user behaviour.
- **Social Media Insights:** Use built-in analytics tools on platforms like Facebook and Twitter.
- **BuzzSumo:** Analyse the social performance of your content and competitors'.

Leveraging Influencer Marketing for Social SEO

Influencers can amplify your social signals by sharing your content with their established audiences.

Steps to Collaborate with Influencers:
1. Identify influencers relevant to your industry.
2. Reach out with a personalized pitch and value proposition.
3. Co-create engaging content, such as product reviews, sponsored posts, or live events.

Avoiding Common Social Media Mistakes

1. Neglecting Mobile Optimization
Most social media users access platforms on mobile devices. Ensure your content and linked pages are mobile-friendly.

2. Overloading with Keywords
Use keywords naturally in your social media captions and bios. Keyword stuffing can make your posts look spammy.

3. Ignoring Negative Comments
Respond to criticism professionally to maintain your brand's credibility.

4. Inconsistent Branding
Maintain a consistent tone, style, and branding across all platforms.

Emerging Trends in Social SEO

1. Short-Form Videos

Platforms like TikTok and Instagram Reels are gaining popularity. Utilize these formats to capture attention and drive traffic.

2. Voice Search Optimization

Prepare for increased voice search queries by crafting conversational social media content.

3. Social Commerce

Leverage features like Instagram Shop and Facebook Marketplace to merge SEO with e-commerce strategies.

CONCLUSION

Social media might not directly influence search rankings, but its indirect impact on SEO is undeniable. By creating shareable content, fostering engagement, and strategically leveraging each platform, you can amplify your brand's reach, attract backlinks, and drive meaningful traffic to your website.

CHAPTER 9

Local SEO Strategies

Winning the Local Search Game

Local SEO is a crucial strategy for businesses looking to attract nearby customers and dominate local markets. With the rise of "near me" searches and location-based queries, search engines have adapted to prioritize hyper-local results. Local SEO ensures your business appears in those local searches, increasing visibility, traffic, and revenue.

This chapter delves into the key elements of local SEO, actionable strategies, and tools to help your business thrive in its geographic area.

What is Local SEO?

Local SEO is the practice of optimizing your online presence to attract customers from a specific geographic location. It involves strategies to rank higher in local search results, such as:

- **Google's Local Pack:** The map-based results displayed for local queries.
- **Organic Search Results:** Regular search listings optimized for local intent.
- **Local Directories:** Listings on platforms like Yelp, Bing Places, and Apple Maps.

For example, a search query like "best coffee shop near me" will return results optimized for local SEO.

Why Local SEO Matters

1. Increased Visibility

A strong local SEO strategy ensures your business is prominently featured in local search results.

2. Higher Conversion Rates

Local searches often have high purchase intent. Users searching for "plumbers in New York" are likely to hire a plumber immediately.

3. Competitive Advantage

Outranking competitors in your local area can significantly boost your customer base.

4. Growth of Mobile and Voice Searches

Mobile devices and voice assistants like Siri and Alexa rely heavily on local SEO data to deliver results.

Key Elements of Local SEO

1. Google Business Profile (GBP)

Formerly known as Google My Business, GBP is the cornerstone of local SEO.

Optimization Tips:
- Fill out your profile completely with accurate business details.
- Add high-quality images of your location, products, or services.
- Encourage and respond to customer reviews.
- Use relevant categories and keywords.

2. Local Citations

These are mentions of your business's name, address, and phone number (NAP) on other websites. Consistent and accurate NAP information is critical for local SEO.

Examples of Citations:
- Online directories (Yelp, Yellow Pages).
- Industry-specific sites.
- Social media platforms.

3. Reviews and Ratings

Positive reviews on platforms like Google, Yelp, and TripAdvisor not only build trust but also improve local rankings.

4. Location-Specific Content

Create blog posts, landing pages, and resources tailored to your local audience. For instance, "Top 5 Places to Visit in [City]" can attract local traffic.

5. Mobile Optimization

Since local searches are predominantly conducted on mobile devices, your website must be mobile-friendly.

6. Schema Markup

Implement local business schema to help search engines understand your business location and services.

Winning Local SEO Strategies

1. Optimize Your Google Business Profile
- Add your operating hours, website URL, and contact details.
- Post updates, offers, and events regularly to keep your profile active.
- Use customer reviews and questions to refine your profile content.

2. Target Local Keywords

Incorporate geo-specific keywords into your content. Examples include:

- "Affordable dentists in Miami"
- "Italian restaurants near Central Park"

Use keyword research tools like Google Keyword Planner or Ubersuggest to find local search terms.

3. Create Location Pages

If your business operates in multiple locations, create dedicated pages for each one. Each page should include:

- Address and contact details.
- Unique content tailored to the location.
- Customer testimonials specific to that branch.

4. Leverage Local Link Building

Earn backlinks from local blogs, news outlets, and business directories.

- Sponsor local events or charities.
- Collaborate with local influencers or bloggers.

5. Focus on Reviews and Reputation Management

- Ask satisfied customers for reviews on Google, Yelp, and industry-specific platforms.
- Respond to all reviews, both positive and negative, to show your commitment to customer service.

6. Use Geotags in Images

Add geotags to images uploaded to your website or social media. Geotagging helps search engines associate your business with a specific location.

The Role of Voice Search in Local SEO

Voice search is transforming how users interact with search engines, especially for local queries.

Optimizing for Voice Search:

- Use natural language in your content, focusing on conversational keywords.
- Optimize for questions starting with "Who," "What," "Where," and "How."
- Ensure your website answers common customer queries clearly.

Tools to Enhance Local SEO

1. Google Business Profile Insights

Monitor how users find and interact with your GBP.

2. Moz Local

Automates citation management to ensure consistent NAP information.

3. BrightLocal

Offers comprehensive local SEO analytics and tools.

4. SEMrush

Tracks local keyword rankings and analyses competitors.

5. Yext

Manages business listings across multiple directories.

Common Local SEO Mistakes to Avoid

1. Inconsistent NAP Information

Ensure your name, address, and phone number are consistent across all platforms.

2. Neglecting Mobile Optimization

A non-mobile-friendly site can lose potential local customers.

3. Overlooking Reviews

Ignoring negative reviews or failing to encourage positive ones can harm your reputation.

4. Ignoring Analytics

Use tools to measure your local SEO performance and make data-driven improvements.

Future Trends in Local SEO

1. Hyper-Local Targeting

The focus will shift toward more precise targeting, such as neighbourhoods or streets.

2. Augmented Reality (AR)

AR will play a role in local search experiences, such as virtual tours or directions.

3. AI-Driven Local Search

AI will enhance personalization in local search results, considering user preferences and behaviours.

CONCLUSION

Local SEO is essential for businesses that rely on attracting nearby customers. By optimizing your Google Business Profile, focusing on reviews, and using location-specific content, you can dominate the local search game. Staying consistent, engaging with your audience, and adapting to emerging trends will ensure long-term success in the local market.

CHAPTER 10

SEO Analytics

Measuring, Monitoring, and Mastering Metrics

SEO is not just about optimizing your website; it's about continuously measuring the impact of your efforts and refining your strategies based on performance. In the ever-changing landscape of search engines, analytics serve as your compass, guiding your campaigns toward measurable success. By monitoring the right metrics and interpreting the data correctly, you can master the art of SEO and ensure sustained growth.

This chapter dives into the fundamentals of SEO analytics, explores key tools, and outlines actionable strategies for tracking and improving performance.

Why SEO Analytics Matter

SEO analytics provide insights into:

1. **Performance:** How well your website ranks for target keywords and overall visibility.
2. **User Behaviour:** Understanding how visitors interact with your website.
3. **ROI Tracking:** Assessing the effectiveness of your SEO investments.
4. **Strategy Refinement:** Identifying areas of improvement and capitalizing on opportunities.

Analytics bridge the gap between intuition and data-driven decision-making, allowing marketers to achieve optimal results.

Key Metrics to Measure in SEO Analytics

1. Organic Traffic

This metric reflects the number of visitors coming to your website through organic search results.

- **Why It Matters:** It shows how well your website is optimized for search engines.
- **Tools to Track:** Google Analytics, SEMrush, Ahrefs.

2. Keyword Rankings

Track how your targeted keywords rank on search engine result pages (SERPs).

- **Why It Matters:** Rankings indicate how visible your site is for specific queries.
- **Tools to Track:** Google Search Console, SERPWatcher, Rank Tracker.

3. Click-Through Rate (CTR)

CTR measures the percentage of users who click on your site after seeing it in search results.

- **Why It Matters:** A higher CTR indicates your title tags and meta descriptions are compelling.
- **Tools to Track:** Google Search Console.

4. Bounce Rate

Bounce rate indicates the percentage of visitors who leave your site after viewing only one page.

- **Why It Matters:** A high bounce rate can signal irrelevant content or poor user experience.
- **Tools to Track:** Google Analytics.

5. Backlink Profile

Analyse the number and quality of external websites linking to your site.

- **Why It Matters:** Backlinks are a critical factor in determining your website's authority.
- **Tools to Track:** Ahrefs, Moz, Majestic.

6. Page Load Time

The time it takes for your website to load impacts user experience and search rankings.

- **Why It Matters:** Faster websites retain users and perform better on search engines.
- **Tools to Track:** Google PageSpeed Insights, GTmetrix.

7. Conversion Rate

This metric tracks the percentage of visitors who complete desired actions (e.g., purchases, sign-ups).

- **Why It Matters:** It reflects how effectively your website turns traffic into customers.
- **Tools to Track:** Google Analytics, HubSpot.

8. Mobile Usability

Analyse how mobile-friendly your website is for users.

- **Why It Matters:** Mobile optimization is a significant ranking factor.
- **Tools to Track:** Google's Mobile-Friendly Test, SEMrush.

Essential SEO Analytics Tools

1. Google Analytics

Google Analytics is the gold standard for tracking user behaviour and website performance.

Key Features:

- Track organic traffic, bounce rates, and user demographics.
- Measure goals like conversions and average session durations.

2. Google Search Console

Provides insights into your website's performance on Google.

Key Features:
- Monitor keyword rankings and click-through rates.
- Identify technical issues like crawl errors or indexing problems.

3. SEMrush

An all-in-one SEO tool with robust analytics capabilities.

Key Features:
- Track keyword rankings and competitor performance.
- Analyse backlink profiles and identify gaps.

4. Ahrefs

A powerful platform for monitoring backlinks and organic traffic.

Key Features:
- Perform content gap analysis.
- Audit your website for technical SEO issues.

5. Hotjar

Provides heatmaps and session recordings to understand user behaviour.

Key Features:
- Visualize how users interact with your pages.
- Identify areas where visitors drop off.

Interpreting SEO Analytics for Actionable Insights

1. Identify High-Performing Pages

Use analytics tools to pinpoint pages with high traffic and engagement.

- Optimize these pages further with internal linking and fresh content.

2. Spot Underperforming Keywords

Identify keywords with low rankings and prioritize them for optimization.

- Enhance content relevance and improve on-page SEO for these terms.

3. Evaluate Content Performance

Analyse which blog posts or landing pages generate the most traffic.

- Update or expand on successful content to maintain its relevance.

4. Monitor Traffic Sources

Determine where your traffic is coming from: organic search, social media, or referrals.

- Allocate resources to the most effective channels.

5. Compare Desktop vs. Mobile Performance

Identify discrepancies between desktop and mobile traffic.

- Optimize your mobile experience if performance lags.

Advanced SEO Analytics Techniques

1. Segment Your Traffic

Break down traffic into segments such as:
- New vs. returning visitors.
- Traffic from specific regions or devices.
- Behaviour of users coming from different search queries.

2. Set Up Conversion Tracking

Use Google Analytics to track specific goals, such as:
- Purchases.
- Form submissions.
- Downloads.

3. Analyse User Journeys

Map the paths users take from landing pages to conversions.
- Identify drop-off points and optimize those pages.

4. Conduct A/B Testing

Test different versions of your title tags, meta descriptions, or landing pages.
- Choose the variation that yields better results.

5. Use Predictive Analytics

Tools like AI-driven insights from platforms such as SEMrush or HubSpot can forecast future trends.

Avoiding Common Pitfalls in SEO Analytics

1. Tracking Too Many Metrics

Focus on metrics that align with your business goals to avoid analysis paralysis.

2. Ignoring Data Trends

Periodic fluctuations in traffic are normal; focus on long-term trends.

3. Overlooking Technical Issues

Even strong content won't perform well if your website has unresolved technical issues.

4. Neglecting Competitor Analysis

Your competitors' performance can offer valuable benchmarks for your strategy.

Emerging Trends in SEO Analytics

1. AI-Powered Insights

Artificial intelligence is increasingly used for predictive analytics and identifying trends.

2. Integration of Multiple Data Sources

Combining data from Google Analytics, social media, and CRM systems provides a comprehensive view.

3. Real-Time Analytics

Real-time tracking tools allow instant responses to traffic changes.

4. Privacy-Centric Analytics

As privacy regulations evolve, analytics tools will adapt to provide insights without compromising user data.

CONCLUSION

SEO analytics is an ongoing process that enables you to measure your efforts, adapt to changing algorithms, and refine your strategies for maximum effectiveness. By mastering the tools and techniques outlined in this chapter, you can turn data into actionable insights and achieve long-term SEO success.

CHAPTER 11

Avoiding SEO Pitfalls

Common Mistakes and How to Prevent Them

Even the most well-intentioned SEO strategies can falter when overlooked mistakes undermine their effectiveness. SEO is a dynamic field that demands precision, consistency, and adaptability. While pursuing higher rankings and increased visibility, it's crucial to be aware of common pitfalls that can derail your efforts.

This chapter explores the frequent errors made by marketers and businesses in SEO, their potential impact, and actionable solutions to avoid them.

Why Avoiding SEO Mistakes Matters

Mistakes in SEO can lead to consequences such as:

1. **Lost Traffic:** Rankings can plummet, leading to reduced visibility.
2. **Wasted Resources:** Time and money invested in ineffective strategies.
3. **Penalties:** Violations of search engine guidelines may result in penalties.
4. **Missed Opportunities:** Failure to capitalize on potential growth areas.

Avoiding these errors is critical for maintaining sustainable success in the competitive digital landscape.

Common SEO Mistakes and How to Prevent Them

1. Neglecting Keyword Research

The Mistake: Targeting irrelevant, overly competitive, or insufficiently researched keywords.

Why It Happens:
- Lack of a clear content strategy.
- Over-reliance on assumptions instead of data.

Prevention Tips:

- Use tools like Google Keyword Planner, SEMrush, or Ahrefs to identify high-value keywords.
- Focus on long-tail keywords with moderate competition and clear intent.
- Regularly review and update your keyword strategy based on analytics.

2. Ignoring Mobile Optimization

The Mistake: Designing a website that performs poorly on mobile devices.

Why It Happens:

- Failing to prioritize mobile users, despite their growing dominance.

Prevention Tips:

- Use responsive design to ensure your site adapts to all screen sizes.
- Test your site's performance using Google's Mobile-Friendly Test.
- Optimize for speed, as mobile users expect fast-loading pages.

3. Overloading Keywords (Keyword Stuffing)

The Mistake: Overusing keywords unnaturally in content.

Why It Happens:

- Misguided attempts to manipulate rankings.

Prevention Tips:

- Focus on creating high-quality, user-centric content.
- Use keywords naturally and sparingly, maintaining readability.
- Prioritize latent semantic indexing (LSI) keywords for variety.

4. Overlooking Technical SEO

The Mistake: Failing to address site speed, crawlability, or indexing issues.

Why It Happens:

- Lack of technical expertise.
- Delayed site audits.

Prevention Tips:

- Conduct regular technical audits with tools like Screaming Frog or SEMrush.
- Fix broken links, ensure proper XML sitemaps, and optimize robots.txt files.
- Enhance site speed by compressing images and leveraging browser caching.

5. Creating Thin or Duplicate Content

The Mistake: Publishing content that lacks depth or originality.

Why It Happens:

- Rushing to produce a high volume of content.
- Copying content without proper credit or value addition.

Prevention Tips:

- Create comprehensive, unique, and engaging content tailored to your audience.
- Use plagiarism checkers to ensure originality.
- Regularly update outdated content with fresh insights.

6. Neglecting Backlink Quality

The Mistake: Pursuing quantity over quality in link-building efforts.

Why It Happens:

- Misguided belief that all backlinks are beneficial.

Prevention Tips:

- Focus on earning backlinks from authoritative, relevant websites.
- Avoid link farms and paid link schemes that violate Google guidelines.
- Use tools like Ahrefs or Moz to audit your backlink profile.

7. Failing to Optimize Meta Tags

The Mistake: Ignoring title tags, meta descriptions, and header tags.

Why It Happens:

- Overlooking their importance in on-page SEO.

Prevention Tips:

- Write compelling, keyword-optimized title tags and meta descriptions.
- Use header tags (H1, H2, etc.) to structure your content for readability and SEO.
- Avoid duplicating meta tags across pages.

8. Not Monitoring Analytics

The Mistake: Launching SEO campaigns without tracking their performance.

Why It Happens:

- Over-reliance on intuition or guesswork.

Prevention Tips:

- Use Google Analytics and Google Search Console to monitor traffic, rankings, and conversions.
- Set clear KPIs to evaluate the success of your campaigns.
- Regularly review data to identify trends and make informed adjustments.

9. Overlooking Local SEO

The Mistake: Failing to optimize for location-specific searches.

Why It Happens:
- Assuming local SEO is unnecessary for online businesses.

Prevention Tips:
- Claim and optimize your Google Business Profile (GBP).
- Encourage customer reviews and manage them actively.
- Incorporate local keywords and create location-specific content.

10. Forgetting About User Experience (UX)

The Mistake: Neglecting site navigation, design, or functionality.

Why It Happens:
- Focusing solely on search engines instead of end-users.

Prevention Tips:
- Simplify navigation with intuitive menus and internal linking.
- Test your website on various devices and browsers.
- Ensure CTAs (Call to Actions) are clear and strategically placed.

SEO Mistakes During Algorithm Updates

1. Ignoring Algorithm Changes

Search engines like Google regularly update their algorithms, which can impact rankings.

Prevention Tips:
- Stay informed through reliable SEO news sources and communities.
- Adapt your strategies to align with new ranking factors.

2. Overreacting to Fluctuations

Sudden drops in rankings can often be temporary.

Prevention Tips:
- Analyse data to identify if changes are due to updates or internal issues.
- Avoid drastic measures; focus on long-term strategies.

SEO Recovery: Fixing Past Mistakes

If your website has suffered due to past mistakes, follow these recovery steps:

1. **Conduct a Full SEO Audit:** Identify technical, on-page, and off-page issues.

2. **Disavow Toxic Backlinks:** Use Google's Disavow Tool to remove harmful links.
3. **Update Outdated Content:** Add new insights, statistics, and visuals.
4. **Rebuild Trust:** Focus on quality content and ethical SEO practices.

Future-Proofing Your SEO Strategy

1. **Adopt a User-First Approach:** Search engines prioritize user satisfaction.
2. **Embrace Emerging Technologies:** Voice search, AI, and machine learning are shaping SEO.
3. **Regularly Review Your Strategy:** Continuously refine your approach based on analytics.

CONCLUSION

Avoiding common SEO mistakes is critical to maintaining a strong online presence. By understanding these pitfalls and implementing preventive measures, you can stay ahead of the competition and maximize the return on your SEO investments.

CHAPTER 12

Advanced Link Building Tactics for Sustainable Growth

Link building is one of the most impactful aspects of off-page SEO. While creating high-quality content is essential, backlinks act as endorsements, signalling to search engines that your site is authoritative and trustworthy. However, in today's SEO landscape, not all backlinks are created equal, and traditional tactics no longer suffice. To achieve sustainable growth, you need a modern, strategic approach to link building.

This chapter explores advanced tactics that prioritize quality, relevance, and long-term benefits, helping you build a robust backlink profile that drives consistent traffic and rankings.

The Evolution of Link Building

In the early days of SEO, link quantity often outweighed quality. However, search engine algorithms, particularly Google's, have evolved to prioritize links from authoritative, relevant sources. This shift underscores the need for strategic link-building methods that align with today's best practices.

Key Principles of Modern Link Building:

1. **Relevance:** Links must come from content and domains related to your niche.
2. **Authority:** High domain authority (DA) sites carry more weight in rankings.
3. **Diversity:** A healthy backlink profile features links from varied sources.
4. **Natural Growth:** Avoid sudden spikes in link acquisition, which may trigger penalties.

Advanced Link Building Tactics

1. The Skyscraper Technique

Overview:
This technique involves identifying popular content in your niche, creating a better version, and reaching out to sites linking to the original.

Steps to Execute:

1. Use tools like Ahrefs or SEMrush to find high-performing content with backlinks.
2. Create content that is more comprehensive, updated, or visually appealing.
3. Reach out to sites linking to the original and pitch your improved resource.

Why It Works: People prefer linking to content that offers more value to their audience.

2. Resource Page Link Building

Overview:
Many websites maintain resource pages linking to helpful tools, guides, or articles.

Steps to Execute:

1. Search for resource pages using queries like "inurl:resources + [your topic]".
2. Identify relevant pages that lack your content.
3. Reach out to the site owner and suggest your content for inclusion.

Why It Works: Resource pages are built to include valuable links, making them ideal for outreach.

3. Broken Link Building

Overview:
This method involves finding broken links on authoritative sites and suggesting your content as a replacement.

Steps to Execute:

1. Use tools like Check My Links (Chrome extension) or Ahrefs to find broken links.
2. Create or identify content on your site that matches the broken link's context.

3. Notify the webmaster about the broken link and recommend your content as an alternative.

Why It Works: Webmasters appreciate being alerted to issues on their sites and are often receptive to helpful suggestions.

4. Digital PR Campaigns

Overview:
Digital PR involves creating newsworthy content or campaigns to attract media coverage and backlinks.

Strategies to Consider:
- Publish original research or data-driven reports.
- Launch a unique campaign, such as an interactive quiz or tool.
- Collaborate with influencers or experts in your niche.

Why It Works: Media outlets and bloggers are always looking for fresh, engaging stories to share.

5. Guest Blogging on Authoritative Sites

Overview:
Contributing articles to high-authority sites in your niche can earn you backlinks and expand your reach.

Steps to Execute:
1. Identify blogs or platforms with a strong readership in your niche.

2. Pitch unique, valuable topics tailored to their audience.
3. Include a natural backlink to your site within the content or author bio.

Why It Works: It positions you as an authority while earning contextual links from reputable sources.

6. Building Linkable Assets

Overview:
Create content specifically designed to attract backlinks, such as:

- Infographics
- Comprehensive guides
- Original studies or data sets

Steps to Execute:

1. Identify gaps in existing resources in your niche.
2. Develop high-quality, shareable content.
3. Promote the content through outreach and social sharing.

Why It Works: Valuable, unique content naturally attracts links from other sites.

7. Partnering with Industry Influencers

Overview:
Collaborate with influencers or thought leaders in your niche to create content or campaigns.

Steps to Execute:

1. Identify influencers who share content similar to yours.
2. Partner on projects such as interviews, co-authored blogs, or webinars.
3. Leverage their audience and relationships to gain backlinks.

Why It Works: Influencers have established authority and can amplify your reach.

8. Leveraging HARO (Help a Reporter Out)

Overview:
HARO connects journalists with experts willing to provide insights for articles.

Steps to Execute:

1. Sign up for HARO and monitor requests relevant to your niche.
2. Respond promptly with valuable, concise insights.
3. Include a link to your site in your response (if permitted).

Why It Works: You can earn backlinks from high-authority publications.

Scaling Link Building Efforts

1. Use Automation Wisely

While tools like BuzzStream and Ninja Outreach can streamline outreach, ensure your communication remains personalized.

2. Build Relationships

Nurture long-term relationships with bloggers, journalists, and industry peers to secure ongoing opportunities.

3. Monitor Your Backlink Profile

Regularly analyse your backlinks using tools like Ahrefs or Moz to identify new opportunities and disavow harmful links.

Avoiding Common Link Building Mistakes

1. Purchasing Links

Buying links violates search engine guidelines and can result in severe penalties.

2. Over-Optimizing Anchor Text

Using exact-match keywords excessively can appear unnatural and trigger penalties.

3. Ignoring Relevance

Links from unrelated sites dilute your backlink profile and offer little SEO value.

The Role of Internal Linking in a Strong SEO Strategy

While external links are vital, don't overlook the power of internal linking. Strategically linking to your content improves crawlability, distributes authority, and enhances user experience.

CONCLUSION

Advanced link-building tactics require a strategic approach, focusing on quality over quantity and long-term sustainability. By leveraging the methods outlined in this chapter, you can create a robust backlink profile that enhances your site's authority, boosts rankings, and drives consistent growth.

CHAPTER 13

Algorithm Updates and SEO
Adapting to Google's Changing Landscape

Search engine optimization (SEO) thrives in a landscape defined by constant evolution. Google's search algorithms, at the heart of this environment, undergo hundreds of changes annually. These updates are designed to refine the user experience by improving search relevance, accuracy, and security. For businesses and marketers, staying ahead of these changes is critical to maintaining visibility and authority.

This chapter delves into the intricacies of Google's algorithm updates, how they impact SEO, and actionable strategies to adapt effectively.

Understanding Google's Algorithm Updates

Google's algorithms determine how web pages are ranked in the search engine results pages (SERPs). The search giant continually refines these algorithms to:

1. Enhance the relevance of search results.
2. Penalize manipulative practices.
3. Reward high-quality, user-focused content.

Types of Algorithm Updates:

1. **Core Updates:** Major changes that affect rankings across the board.
2. **Targeted Updates:** Focus on specific areas, such as page speed or mobile usability.
3. **Spam Updates:** Aim to penalize low-quality or manipulative content.

Notable Algorithm Updates and Their Impact

1. Panda Update (2011)

Focus: Content quality.
- Penalized thin, duplicate, or low-quality content.
- Rewarded well-researched, in-depth content.

Key Adaptations:
- Prioritize unique, comprehensive content.

- Eliminate duplicate or low-value pages from your site.

2. Penguin Update (2012)

Focus: Backlink quality.

- Penalized sites using manipulative link-building tactics, such as link farms or paid links.

Key Adaptations:

- Conduct regular backlink audits.
- Disavow spammy or low-quality links.
- Focus on earning natural, authoritative backlinks.

3. Hummingbird Update (2013)

Focus: Semantic search and user intent.

- Improved Google's ability to understand search queries beyond exact keywords.

Key Adaptations:

- Emphasize context and intent in content creation.
- Incorporate long-tail keywords and natural language.

4. Mobile-Friendly Update (2015)

Focus: Mobile usability.

- Prioritized mobile-optimized sites in mobile search results.

Key Adaptations:
- Use responsive design for seamless mobile experiences.
- Optimize page speed and navigation for mobile users.

5. RankBrain (2015)

Focus: Machine learning and user behaviour.
- Considered factors like click-through rate (CTR) and dwell time in rankings.

Key Adaptations:
- Craft compelling meta titles and descriptions to improve CTR.
- Create engaging content to increase dwell time.

6. BERT Update (2019)

Focus: Natural language processing (NLP).
- Enhanced Google's understanding of context and nuances in search queries.

Key Adaptations:
- Write for humans, not search engines.
- Address user questions comprehensively.

Staying Ahead of Algorithm Updates

1. Focus on User Experience (UX)

Algorithm updates consistently prioritize user satisfaction.

Best Practices:
- Ensure fast page load times.
- Create intuitive navigation structures.
- Optimize for mobile and desktop users.

2. Emphasize High-Quality Content

Content remains the cornerstone of SEO, irrespective of algorithm changes.

Best Practices:
- Publish in-depth, accurate, and engaging content.
- Regularly update outdated content to maintain relevance.
- Use multimedia elements like images, videos, and infographics to enhance value.

3. Build a Diverse Backlink Profile

Quality backlinks remain a strong ranking factor.

Best Practices:
- Focus on earning links from relevant, authoritative sources.
- Avoid manipulative link-building tactics that could trigger penalties.

4. Stay Informed About Updates

Google often provides insights into upcoming changes.

How to Stay Updated:
- Follow official sources like Google Search Central and Webmaster Blog.
- Join SEO communities and forums.
- Monitor tools like Moz, Ahrefs, and SEMrush for changes in rankings.

Responding to Algorithm Changes

1. Conduct an Impact Assessment

Determine how the update has affected your site.

Steps:
- Analyse fluctuations in rankings, traffic, and conversions.
- Use Google Analytics and Search Console to identify affected pages.

2. Audit Your Website

Identify areas that need improvement.

Focus Areas:
- Content quality and relevance.
- Backlink profile health.
- Technical SEO issues like crawl errors or duplicate content.

3. Adjust Your Strategy

Align your approach with the new ranking factors.

Key Actions:
- Optimize content to meet updated guidelines.
- Address technical issues that hinder performance.
- Double down on user-focused strategies.

Preparing for Future Updates

1. Adopt a Holistic SEO Approach

Focusing on one aspect of SEO is no longer sufficient.

Key Areas to Integrate:
- On-page and technical SEO.
- Content marketing and link building.
- Mobile and local SEO strategies.

2. Embrace Emerging Technologies

AI, voice search, and visual search are shaping the future of SEO.

Action Plan:
- Optimize content for voice search with conversational keywords.
- Implement structured data for enhanced search visibility.
- Stay updated on AI-driven tools and trends.

3. Regularly Audit Your Site

Frequent audits ensure your site remains optimized for evolving algorithms.

What to Review:
- Page speed and usability.
- Backlink profile for toxic links.
- Content for freshness and accuracy.

CONCLUSION

Google's algorithm updates are a testament to the ever-evolving nature of search engines. By understanding their purpose, impact, and best practices, you can adapt your SEO strategies to thrive in a competitive landscape. Staying informed, focusing on quality, and embracing change are the keys to sustaining success in the dynamic world of SEO.

CHAPTER 14

Creating an Effective SEO Strategy
Planning for Long-Term Success

A successful SEO strategy is not about short-term wins but about building sustainable growth that aligns with your business goals. With search engine algorithms constantly evolving and competition increasing, a well-thought-out SEO plan is essential for achieving long-term visibility and authority in search engine results pages (SERPs).

This chapter provides a comprehensive guide to developing an effective, future-proof SEO strategy. By integrating technical, on-page, off-page, and content-focused techniques into a cohesive plan, you can ensure consistent growth in traffic, rankings, and user engagement.

Understanding the Importance of Strategic SEO Planning

An effective SEO strategy bridges the gap between your business objectives and search engine optimization. Instead of chasing temporary gains, a strategic approach allows you to:

- Build authority and trust over time.
- Adapt to algorithm updates without losing rankings.
- Optimize resources by focusing on high-impact activities.

Key Elements of a Strong SEO Strategy:

1. **Clear Objectives:** What do you want to achieve? (e.g., increased traffic, higher conversions)
2. **Data-Driven Insights:** Use analytics and keyword research to guide decisions.
3. **Comprehensive Execution:** Cover all facets of SEO, from technical to content creation.
4. **Continuous Improvement:** Regularly review and refine your approach.

Step-by-Step Guide to Creating an SEO Strategy

1. Define Your Goals

Your goals should align with your broader business objectives. Consider:

- **Traffic Goals:** How many users do you aim to attract per month?
- **Engagement Goals:** Are users spending more time on your site or exploring multiple pages?
- **Conversion Goals:** Are you achieving sales, sign-ups, or other desired actions?

SMART Goals: Ensure your objectives are Specific, Measurable, Achievable, Relevant, and Time-bound.

2. Conduct a Comprehensive SEO Audit

Before planning, evaluate your current performance.

Key Areas to Assess:
- **Technical SEO:** Analyse site speed, crawlability, and mobile responsiveness.
- **Content Quality:** Identify gaps, outdated posts, and underperforming pages.
- **Backlink Profile:** Review your inbound links for quality and relevance.
- **Keyword Rankings:** Determine which keywords are driving traffic and where you lag behind.

Use tools like Google Search Console, Ahrefs, and SEMrush to gather insights.

3. Research and Prioritize Keywords

Keyword research is the foundation of SEO strategy. Focus on finding terms that match user intent and align with your business.

Approach:
1. Use tools like Google Keyword Planner and Ubersuggest to generate ideas.
2. Identify **low-competition, high-volume** keywords for quick wins.
3. Prioritize long-tail keywords for niche targeting.
4. Map keywords to specific content pieces or pages.

Tip: Don't just target competitive keywords; find opportunities in underserved areas.

4. Develop a Content Marketing Plan

Content is the vehicle that delivers your SEO efforts to users. High-quality, optimized content not only attracts search engines but also engages visitors.

Key Steps:
1. Create a content calendar with topics based on keyword research.
2. Include diverse content types (blogs, videos, infographics, case studies).
3. Address user intent: informational, transactional, and navigational.
4. Regularly update older content to maintain relevance.

Pro Tip: Use pillar pages and topic clusters to create a strong internal linking structure.

5. Optimize On-Page Elements

On-page optimization ensures your content and pages are search-engine-friendly.

Focus Areas:
- **Meta Tags:** Create compelling title tags and meta descriptions.
- **Headers:** Use H1s, H2s, and H3s to structure content effectively.
- **URLs:** Keep URLs short, descriptive, and keyword-rich.
- **Internal Links:** Link to related content to improve navigation and authority.
- **Images:** Optimize file sizes and add alt text for accessibility.

Example:
Instead of using a generic title like "SEO Tips," opt for "15 Proven SEO Tips to Boost Your Rankings in 2024."

6. Strengthen Your Technical SEO

Technical SEO ensures that search engines can easily crawl and index your site.

Best Practices:
- **Improve Page Speed:** Use tools like PageSpeed Insights to optimize load times.

- **Ensure Mobile Usability:** Test responsiveness using Google's Mobile-Friendly Test.
- **Fix Errors:** Resolve broken links, duplicate content, and crawl errors.
- **Secure Your Site:** Enable HTTPS to build user trust and rank higher.

7. Build Authority with Off-Page SEO

Off-page SEO involves strategies that boost your domain authority and credibility.

Tactics:

- **Earn Backlinks:** Focus on quality over quantity by pursuing links from reputable sites.
- **Engage on Social Media:** Share content and interact with your audience to build social signals.
- **Collaborate:** Partner with influencers or industry experts for co-marketing opportunities.

8. Leverage Analytics and Reporting

SEO is a data-driven discipline. Regularly monitor performance to identify strengths and weaknesses.

Tools to Use:

- **Google Analytics:** Track traffic, user behaviour, and conversions.
- **Search Console:** Monitor indexing, errors, and keyword performance.
- **Third-Party Tools:** Use SEMrush or Ahrefs for competitor analysis and backlink tracking.

Metrics to Measure:
- Organic traffic growth.
- Bounce rate and dwell time.
- Conversion rates from search traffic.
- Rankings for target keywords.

Adapting Your Strategy Over Time

An effective SEO strategy is never static. Keep your plan agile by:
1. Staying updated on algorithm changes and SEO trends.
2. Experimenting with new tactics and evaluating their impact.
3. Regularly revisiting and revising your goals based on performance data.

Case Study: Long-Term Success in SEO

Scenario: A small e-commerce brand increased its organic traffic by 150% in two years.

Steps Taken:
- Conducted thorough keyword research to identify untapped opportunities.
- Focused on creating content around buyer intent keywords.
- Partnered with industry bloggers for high-authority backlinks.
- Regularly optimized product pages for speed and mobile usability.
Outcome: Consistent growth in traffic, improved SERP rankings, and a higher conversion rate.

CONCLUSION

Creating an effective SEO strategy requires patience, persistence, and adaptability. By aligning your efforts with a clear vision, prioritizing user-focused techniques, and staying informed about industry trends, you can secure long-term success in the competitive world of SEO.

CHAPTER 15

Future Trends in SEO

Staying Ahead in a Competitive Digital World

The digital landscape evolves at a staggering pace, with SEO trends continuously reshaping how businesses optimize for search engines. Staying competitive requires not just adapting to current practices but anticipating future changes. As technology advances and user behaviour shifts, SEO professionals must embrace innovation, agility, and forward-thinking strategies to maintain relevance and achieve sustainable growth.

This final chapter examines emerging trends in SEO, the role of new technologies, and actionable steps to future-proof your strategy. By understanding where the industry is heading, you can position your website for success in an ever-changing digital world.

The Drivers of SEO Evolution

Several factors influence the direction of SEO trends. Understanding these drivers helps contextualize the future of optimization:

1. **Advancements in AI and Machine Learning:** Tools like Google's RankBrain and BERT use AI to deliver better search results, emphasizing relevance and intent over exact keywords.
2. **Voice Search and Conversational AI:** Devices like Alexa and Google Assistant have made voice search a standard part of how users interact with search engines.
3. **Visual Search:** Innovations like Google Lens allow users to search using images instead of text.
4. **Mobile-First Indexing:** With the majority of searches originating from mobile devices, Google continues to prioritize mobile usability.
5. **Privacy and Data Regulations:** Growing concerns around data privacy are influencing how search engines collect and process user information.

Emerging SEO Trends

1. AI-Driven Optimization

Artificial intelligence is shaping how search engines analyse content and deliver results.

Impact on SEO:
- Content needs to be more contextually relevant and user-focused.

- AI-powered tools like Jasper and ChatGPT are enabling marketers to create high-quality content more efficiently.

Action Steps:

- Leverage AI for predictive analytics and keyword insights.
- Use tools like Clearscope to align content with AI-driven search engine priorities.

2. Zero-Click Searches and Featured Snippets

Search engines aim to provide users with answers directly on the SERPs, reducing the need for clicks.

Impact on SEO:

- Featured snippets, People Also Ask boxes, and knowledge panels dominate SERPs.
- Websites must optimize for these elements to maintain visibility.

Action Steps:

- Structure content with clear headings and concise answers.
- Use schema markup to increase the chances of being featured.

3. Voice Search Optimization

Voice search is growing rapidly as users seek faster, hands-free ways to find information.

Impact on SEO:

- Voice queries are often longer and conversational.
- Local search and question-based content are becoming more important.

Action Steps:

- Optimize for long-tail, natural-language keywords.
- Ensure your site is mobile-friendly and loads quickly to improve voice search rankings.

4. The Rise of Visual Search

Visual search tools allow users to search by uploading images or using live cameras.

Impact on SEO:

- Image optimization becomes more critical than ever.
- Ecommerce sites benefit significantly from visual search features.

Action Steps:

- Use high-quality images with descriptive file names and alt text.
- Implement structured data to enhance visual search capabilities.

5. Content Experience and Personalization

Search engines increasingly prioritize content that meets individual user needs.

Impact on SEO:

- Personalized search results based on user history, preferences, and location.
- A focus on delivering value rather than merely targeting keywords.

Action Steps:

- Use dynamic content strategies to tailor experiences for different audience segments.
- Leverage analytics to understand user behaviour and refine your content strategy.

6. Emphasis on E-A-T (Expertise, Authoritativeness, Trustworthiness)

Google's algorithms prioritize content that demonstrates expertise, authority, and trustworthiness.

Impact on SEO:

- Businesses must establish credibility to rank higher.
- Content from verified experts is favoured.

Action Steps:

- Showcase author credentials and expertise.
- Secure backlinks from authoritative sites.
- Keep information accurate and up to date.

Technologies Shaping the Future of SEO

1. Augmented Reality (AR) and Virtual Reality (VR)

AR and VR technologies are increasingly integrated into search experiences, particularly for retail and real estate.

Example: Virtual try-on tools for products directly in search results.

Action Steps:
- Experiment with AR/VR integrations to enhance user engagement.
- Optimize content for AR-supported search platforms.

2. Blockchain Technology

Blockchain's decentralized nature is reshaping data security and transparency in SEO.

Potential Impact:
- New forms of ad tracking and attribution.
- Increased trust in verified content.

Action Steps:
- Stay informed about blockchain applications in digital marketing.

- Explore partnerships with platforms utilizing blockchain for content authenticity.

Adapting to Future SEO Trends

To stay competitive, businesses must embrace a proactive and flexible approach to SEO.

1. Monitor Industry Changes

Regularly track updates from Google and other search engines.

Resources:
- Google Search Central Blog.
- Industry tools like SEMrush and Moz.
- Networking with SEO communities and forums.

2. Test and Experiment

SEO strategies should evolve through experimentation.

Examples:
- A/B test content formats and CTAs.
- Pilot new tools like AI-driven content creators.

3. Prioritize User Intent and Experience

Search engines increasingly reward websites that provide value and excellent user experiences.

Key Areas to Optimize:
- Page speed and mobile responsiveness.
- Accessibility and navigability.
- Content that addresses user questions and solves problems.

Looking Ahead: The Future of SEO

SEO is transitioning from being a technical discipline to a user-centric art form. As algorithms evolve to mimic human understanding, success lies in providing authentic, valuable, and seamless user experiences. By integrating advanced technologies and adapting to user behaviour, businesses can maintain a competitive edge in the digital realm.

The next steps for your journey as an SEO professional are clear: Stay informed, embrace innovation, and never stop learning. The future of SEO is bright for those who plan ahead and adapt swiftly to the changing tides.

CONCLUSION CHAPTER

Mastering SEO

Final Thoughts and Expert Advice from Zaheer Ahmed Shaik

As we conclude this comprehensive guide, it's essential to reflect on the key takeaways from each chapter and synthesize them into actionable insights for your SEO journey. Search engine optimization is not merely a set of techniques but an evolving discipline that bridges technology, content, and human intent.

Drawing from the wealth of information shared throughout this book, this chapter provides final thoughts, invaluable advice, and expert tips to empower you to achieve sustained SEO success. As Zaheer Ahmed Shaik, a seasoned business consultant and SEO expert, I aim to leave you with a blueprint for mastering SEO in a competitive digital landscape.

Reflections on SEO: A Holistic Approach

SEO requires a multifaceted approach that combines technical precision, creative content, and strategic thinking. To thrive in this ever-changing field, always remember these core principles:

1. **User-Centric Optimization:** Search engines are built to serve users, not websites. Prioritize user needs and experiences at every stage of your strategy.
2. **Adaptability:** SEO is a dynamic field influenced by trends, algorithms, and technology. Stay informed and be ready to pivot.
3. **Patience and Consistency:** Achieving lasting results takes time. Focus on sustainable growth rather than quick wins.

Expert Advice for Best SEO Practices

1. Lay a Strong Foundation
- Conduct a thorough **SEO audit** regularly to identify strengths and weaknesses.
- Prioritize mobile responsiveness and page speed as foundational elements.
- Ensure your website's architecture is clear, accessible, and crawlable.

2. Master the Art of Keyword Research
- Go beyond basic keyword tools—leverage advanced platforms like Ahrefs and SEMrush for deeper insights.
- Focus on **user intent** when selecting keywords: are users seeking information, making comparisons, or ready to buy?
- Revisit and update your keyword strategy periodically to align with market shifts.

3. Create Exceptional Content

- Embrace the philosophy of "content is king." Craft content that educates, entertains, and inspires action.
- Use storytelling techniques to connect with your audience emotionally while addressing their pain points.
- Integrate keywords naturally—avoid overstuffing or compromising readability.

4. Optimize for Technical Excellence

- Regularly monitor for **crawl errors**, broken links, and duplicate content.
- Use schema markup to improve how search engines interpret your content.
- Keep your site secure with HTTPS to enhance trustworthiness and ranking potential.

5. Build a Strong Backlink Profile

- Focus on acquiring backlinks from authoritative and relevant websites.
- Build relationships within your industry through guest posting, collaborations, and partnerships.
- Avoid black-hat tactics like link farming or purchasing backlinks—they can result in penalties.

6. Leverage Analytics to Refine Your Strategy

- Use tools like Google Analytics and Search Console to track performance.
- Identify high-performing content and replicate its success.
- Regularly monitor key metrics like organic traffic, bounce rate, and conversion rates.

7. Stay Ahead with Emerging Trends

- Optimize for **voice and visual search**, as they are transforming how users interact with search engines.
- Invest in **AI-powered tools** for content creation, keyword analysis, and audience targeting.
- Keep a close eye on algorithm updates and adjust your strategies accordingly.

Guidelines from Zaheer Ahmed Shaik for Long-Term SEO Success

1. **Be Authentic:** Search engines reward genuine efforts to provide value. Avoid manipulative practices that undermine trust.
2. **Stay Educated:** Attend webinars, follow SEO thought leaders, and read authoritative blogs to keep your knowledge current.
3. **Experiment and Innovate:** Don't hesitate to test new strategies or tools. Innovation often leads to breakthroughs.
4. **Align SEO with Business Goals:** Every optimization effort should contribute to broader objectives like brand awareness, lead generation, or revenue growth.
5. **Focus on Local SEO:** For businesses with a physical presence, optimizing for local searches can significantly boost visibility and customer acquisition.

Inspiration for the Future

SEO is a journey, not a destination. As the digital ecosystem continues to grow and evolve, your role as a marketer, business owner, or SEO professional is to remain curious, resilient, and adaptable.

Remember, success in SEO is not measured solely by rankings or traffic but by the value you provide to your audience and the relationships you build along the way.

Closing Note from the Author

As a business consultant and SEO expert, my mission has always been to empower individuals and businesses to thrive in the digital era. This book is a culmination of years of experience, research, and a deep understanding of what works and what doesn't in SEO.

I encourage you to revisit these chapters often, use them as a guide, and implement the strategies step by step. SEO success is within your reach—it requires determination, creativity, and a commitment to continuous learning.

Thank you for embarking on this journey with me. May your efforts lead to unparalleled growth, visibility, and impact in the competitive digital world.

With best wishes,
Zaheer Ahmed Shaik

REFERENCES

This book, ***Mastering SEO Excellence: Proven On-Page and Off-Page Strategies for Top SERP Rankings***, is a comprehensive guide compiled using insights, expertise, and information drawn from years of professional experience, industry trends, and reputable resources. Below is a curated list of references that provided foundational knowledge, data, and inspiration for this book:

Books and Textbooks

1. **Search Engine Optimization All-in-One For Dummies** by Bruce Clay
2. **The Art of SEO: Mastering Search Engine Optimization** by Eric Enge, Stephan Spencer, and Jessie Stricchiola
3. **SEO 2024: Learn Search Engine Optimization with Smart Internet Marketing Strategies** by Adam Clarke
4. **Content Chemistry: The Illustrated Handbook for Content Marketing** by Andy Crestodina
5. **SEO Fitness Workbook: Your Step-by-Step Guide to Dominating Google** by Jason McDonald
6. **Ultimate Guide to Link Building** by Eric Ward and Garrett French

Industry Articles and White Papers

7. Google's Search Engine Optimization (SEO) Starter Guide – Official Google Documentation
8. MOZ Beginner's Guide to SEO – MOZ.com
9. Backlinko's Complete Guide to SEO – Backlinko.com (Brian Dean)

10. SEMrush White Papers and Research Reports – SEMrush.com

11. Ahrefs Blog and SEO Tutorials – Ahrefs.com

12. Search Engine Journal Articles – SEJ.com

13. Neil Patel's Advanced SEO Insights – NeilPatel.com

Online Tools and Platforms Consulted

14. Google Search Console and Analytics Documentation

15. Ahrefs Keyword Research and Competitive Analysis Tools

16. SEMrush SEO Toolkit and Reports

17. Ubersuggest for Keyword Insights and Trends

18. Screaming Frog SEO Spider for Technical SEO Auditing

19. Yoast SEO Tutorials and Resources

Web Resources and Blogs

20. HubSpot's SEO Hub and Knowledge Base – HubSpot.com

21. Hootsuite Blog on Social Signals and SEO – Hootsuite.com

22. BrightLocal Blog for Local SEO Tips – BrightLocal.com

23. Search Engine Land – Daily Updates and News on SEO

Personal Case Studies and Experiences

24. Projects and case studies conducted by **Zaheer Ahmed Shaik** as part of professional SEO consulting services.

25. Real-world applications and strategies tested and implemented for various businesses in diverse industries, including health, retail, and technology.

Additional Academic and Industry Journals

26. Journal of Marketing Research – Published works on digital marketing strategies.

27. Harvard Business Review – Insights into marketing and technology intersections.

28. Digital Marketing Institute – Trends and certifications in SEO and digital marketing.